Dear Fr...

We'd like to take this opportunity to personally thank you for visiting one of our many offices to pick up this cook book. May it provide you, your family and friends many hours of pleasant dining.

We hope this book will always remind you that there is ALWAYS something "cooking" at American Savings. We can provide you with the highest quality ingredients available to anyone, including:

★ **SAFETY SINCE 1885**

★ **ASSETS OVER 5½ <u>BILLION</u> DOLLARS STRONG**

★ **NATION'S <u>HIGHEST INTEREST</u> ON INSURED SAVINGS**

★ **LOWER YOUR INCOME TAXES WITH RETIREMENT PLANS**

★ **MANY FREE SERVICES WITH SPECIFIED MINIMUM BALANCES**

★ **OVER 70 CONVENIENT LOCATIONS**

★ **FRIENDLIEST PEOPLE TO SERVE YOU**

We know you will find these ingredients to your liking, and that is why American Savings is one of the NATION'S LARGEST financial institutions.

Remember, at American Savings YOU *NEVER* LOSE, YOU *ALWAYS* GAIN! And, *Bon App*étit!

Sincerely,

W. J. Popejoy   *S. Mark Taper*

William J. Popejoy
President

S. Mark Taper
Chairman of the Board

AMERICAN SAVINGS AND LOAN ASSOCIATION

❧❧❧

MICHELE EVANS' ALL POULTRY COOKBOOK

A Dell Book

Published by
Dell Publishing Co., Inc.
1 Dag Hammarskjold Plaza
New York, New York 10017

Dell ® TM 681510, Dell Publishing Co., Inc.
Printed in the United States of America
First printing—February 1974
Second printing—June 1974
Third printing—July 1976

For all my family,
with love

CONTENTS

INTRODUCTION

A chicken or turkey cooking in the kitchen has always made me eager for dinner, so testing and writing these All Poultry recipes was a special treat for me.

There are hundreds of recipes for preparing fowl, and for one excellent reason: it lends itself to so many ways of cooking. Then too, the fowl is most accommodating. It is almost as if all sorts of herbs, spices, and vegetables were discovered especially to make the bird—be it domestic or wild—that much more enticing.

Baked Chicken with Cheese and Onions, Chicken Kiev, Chicken Tandoori, Coq au Vin, Duck with Pineapple and Sausage Stuffing, Goose with Onions and Sage—if one were to challenge a selection, these then are my favorites. But I have used and enjoyed all of the recipes included in this book. Some are simple, others most elaborate. But even those that seem complicated are so only in terms of multiplicity of ingredients or length of time needed to prepare them— none requires perfect timing or formidable cooking feats.

Don't be afraid to experiment with dishes you have never attempted. Cooking should be an enjoyable and rewarding adventure. Organization is important to achieve this happy feeling. Always read the recipe through completely before you begin to cook so the ingredients and utensils will be on hand as they are needed. One of the French chefs I studied with taught me that cleaning up and putting away articles as I finished using them avoided confusion and saved valuable time in the long run. I have tried to make the recipes that follow interesting and clear so they will afford fun for the cook and pleasure to the diner.

MICHELE EVANS

TRUSSING

With Needle:
Chicken and turkey are trussed in the same manner, using a trussing needle and strong thin white kitchen string. (A large turkey will require a longer needle.) Stuff bird before trussing. Push threaded needle through the left thigh and out the other side of right thigh. Next push needle through wings including neck skin folded down in back (fasten it to back with thread) and out through other wing. Now bring needle around to end of drumsticks and pull up parson's nose, wrap thread around and tie securely together.

Without Needle:
A chicken can also be easily trussed without a trussing needle. Just cut a piece of white kitchen string a little over a yard long and place the chicken on it's back with legs pointing away from you. Wind the center of the string under and around the two drumstick ends and cross the drumsticks. Push the drumsticks up against the breast at the vent opening. Pull the string ends along the skin between the legs and sides of the breast. Turn chicken over and bring string through and around the center joint of each wing and tie together in back. Fold each wing tip back. This is the method most butchers use.

CARVING

To carve a turkey or a large bird, place the bird on a carving board, directly in front of the person carving, drumsticks pointed toward him. The serving platter should be right next to the board. Sever leg from body at the joint, remove to serving plate and separate the thigh from the drumstick by cutting at the second joint. Slice the thigh and drumstick into neat pieces for the dark meat. Remove the wing by pressing the wing tip down to reveal the joint and sever it there. Place wing aside and don't serve. Next cut through the breast horizontally so that the breast meat will fall away easily when sliced. Cut into fairly thin slices and continue until you reach the wide part of the breast. Now spoon the stuffing from the cavity onto the platter and serve along with the meat.

NOTE: bird carcass should be saved to make a rich stock. A recipe for stock follows the giblet gravy recipe in this section.

GIBLET GRAVY

    giblets including neck of chicken,
      turkey, or other bird. (Reserve liver)
1 medium-sized onion, chopped
1 stalk celery and leaves, chopped
1 carrot, chopped
3 sprigs parsley
  pinch of thyme
1 bay leaf
1 quart water
1 teaspoon salt
¼ teaspoon pepper
3 tablespoons flour

Place giblets, onion, celery, carrot, parsley, thyme, and bay leaf in saucepan. Add water and salt and pepper; bring to a boil and simmer for 1½ hours. Add liver and simmer for 20 minutes longer. Strain, adjust seasoning. Pour off all but 3 tablespoons drippings from roasting pan where bird has just been roasted. Sprinkle flour over pan and stir vigorously to scrape up any browned particles sticking to pan. Pour in stock, always stirring, until smooth and thickened. (Giblets can be chopped fine and added if desired.) Serve in heated sauceboat.

Yields about 2 cups.

RICH POULTRY STOCK

1 chicken, turkey, or other bird carcass (cut
　　up), neck, and giblets
1 large onion, chopped
2 carrots, chopped
1 turnip, chopped (optional)
2 stalks celery, chopped
1 bouquet garni
½ teaspoon poultry seasoning
2 tablespoons salt
3 quarts cold water

Put ingredients in soup kettle and add cold water.
Bring to a boil, reduce heat, and simmer, partially
covered, for 2½ hours. The longer you cook the
richer the stock.

Strain. Cool, refrigerate, and remove fat.

Makes 2 to 2½ quarts.

WINE SUGGESTIONS

Choosing the appropriate wine—red or white—to accompany a particular dish is a matter that is often subjected to far too rigid standards. To an extent, it is a matter of personal taste. Some rules are sensible: for example, a game bird such as wild duck requires a full-bodied red Burgundy. On the other hand, a simple roast chicken can be served with either red or white wine. The selection also depends on the wine used in preparing the dish—if one is used. Chicken Chablis and Coq au Vin should be accompanied by the same kind of wine that was used in their cooking.

As for serving temperatures: Remember that the rule "red wine should be served at room temperature" was made years ago in Europe when room temperature seldom rose to 72°F. About 65°F. is perfect, so store the wine in a cool part of the house. White wine is best chilled—not ice cold, only champagne is served iced. If you care for rosé, it should be chilled.

Red Bordeaux or Burgundy should be uncorked at least ½ hour before dinner. The more full the wine, the more time it needs to breathe.

The following chart suggests some wines that naturally complement the particular bird mentioned— or the manner of preparation. It is meant only as a general guide. Do some test tasting of your own— and watch for bargains. Be sure to try American wines, some are even more rewarding for the price than the French.

BIRD	COOKING METHOD	WINE
Chicken *Turkey* *Capon* *Cornish game* Hens	in wine sauce	Same wine as used in sauce. Red and white Mâcon wines are very good
	cream sauces	White Burgundy— Chablis Pouilly-Fumé, Pouilly-Fuissé
	cold or poached	Moselle or Rosé
	curried or highly spiced dishes	White Burgundy, Chablis, Mersault
	roast, sautéed, grilled, or fried	Red or White Bordeaux —Médoc, Graves— Sancerre, St. Émilion
Duck	all methods	Full-bodied red—a good Bordeaux—St. Émilion or Burgundy —Châteauneuf-du-Pape, Chambertin
Goose	all methods	White Burgundy or Alsatian wines
Quail *Squab* *Pigeon*	all methods	White or Red Bordeaux—Italian wines, Soave, Valpolicella

BIRD	COOKING METHOD	WINE
Game Birds	all methods	Full-bodied Red Bordeaux—St. Émilion or Burgundy —Pomerol, Corton, Châteauneuf-du-Pape

CHICKEN

Tasty, versatile, economical—no wonder chicken is so popular. Available all year long, it can be used for nearly every course in a meal: appetizer, soup, salad, sandwich, entrée. And it can be broiled, grilled, roasted, poached, baked, fried, sautéed, or fricasseed. Chicken is an excellent source of protein, and dieters are fond of it because a serving contains fewer calories than comparable servings of most other meats. Whole birds or cut-up chicken pieces are plentiful in modern markets. Buying a whole bird and cutting it into serving pieces saves on the cost, since cut-up parts are usually a few cents higher. Either whole or in parts, the chicken should have an official United States Department of Agriculture inspection mark and grade "A" tag. Such marks will not appear on fresh birds of course.

Prepackaged fowl cannot compare in tenderness or flavor with the meat of a fresh-killed bird. Fresh chicken should be cooked as soon as possible, and as simply as possible: a bit of butter and a touch of tarragon is all a fresh chicken needs to enhance it. There are still butcher shops and farms where fresh-killed birds can be purchased, but they are rare. Treasure the butcher or farmer who provides the fresh chicken and encourage him to stay in business.

To select a chicken look for smooth, moist skin, a full breast, and a flexible breastbone. Beware of bruised, purplish, dry, or torn skin. Chicken is highly perishable and will keep only one or two days in the refrigerator.

Frozen chicken can be kept safely in your freezer for as long as three or four months. To thaw, leave it in the refrigerator overnight or place (in its original wrapping) under cold water for a few hours. Cook soon after thawing.

The recipes that follow should prove the infinite variety offered by this humble domestic bird—everything from a quick snack to those special treats that add elegance to the table when an occasion is at hand or company at the door.

Chickens are classified according to age, which dictates how they will be cooked.

CHICKEN	READY TO COOK WEIGHT	METHODS OF COOKING
Broiler (10 to 14 weeks old)	1½ to 2½ pounds	Broil or grill
Fryer (14 to 20 weeks old)	2½ to 3½ pounds	Fry, sauté, roast, poach, fricassee, for casserole
Capon (7 to 10 months)	5 to 8 pounds	Roast, fricassee, poach, for casserole
Stewing Chicken, Mature Chicken or *Fowl* (11 months or older)	3 to 6 pounds	Stew or fricassee

CHICKEN AS
AN APPEALING APPETIZER

Chicken appetizers are welcomed because they are both temptingly flavorful and unusually substantial. They provide more than the traditional tidbit for the snacking cocktail guest. And, as a first course, they are delicious without overpowering the rest of the meal. What could be more impressive or enticing to the appetite than a slice of chicken quiche or a helping of chicken mousse?

APPETIZER CHICKEN STICKS

- 12 chicken wings
- ¾ cup flour
- 1 teaspoon paprika
- 1 teaspoon dried basil
- 1 teaspoon dried parsley
- 1 teaspoon dried oregano
- ½ cup fresh grated Parmesan or Romano cheese
- 1 teaspoon salt
- pepper to taste
- 1 cup heavy cream
- oil for deep-fat frying

Cut pinions off wings and save for stock or discard. Cut remaining two sections of wing in half, making 24 pieces of chicken. In bowl mix together dry ingredients. Dip each chicken piece in heavy cream and roll in herbed flour–cheese mixture. Heat oil and deep-fat-fry several chicken sticks at a time, approximately 8 to 10 minutes. Turn several times during cooking. Drain.

Serves 6 to 8 as an appetizer.

CHICKEN BALLS

    2 chicken breasts, skinned and boned
    1 medium onion
    3 eggs
    ½ cup bread crumbs
    2 cloves garlic, crushed
    2 tablespoons minced green pepper
    ½ teaspoon salt
    ¼ teaspoon pepper
      flour
      bread crumbs
      oil

Grind chicken and onion in meat grinder and mix with 1 egg, ½ cup bread crumbs, garlic, green pepper, salt and pepper. Refrigerate for ½ hour. Form into bite-size balls and roll in flour, then dip in beaten eggs. Coat with bread crumbs and fry in heated oil until golden all over. Serve with toothpicks.

Appetizer for 6 to 8.

CHICKEN BREAST APPETIZER

3 whole chicken breasts, skinned, boned, and cut
    into small pieces about 1 inch square
  flour
  salt and pepper
1 stick butter or 4 ounces
2 tablespoons oil

DIP

1 cup mayonnaise
1 tablespoon curry powder
1 tablespoon fresh lemon juice

Dredge chicken in flour that has been seasoned with salt and pepper. Melt butter and add oil. Sauté chicken a few pieces at a time until golden on all sides. Transfer chicken pieces to heated platter as they are cooked. Blend together ingredients of dip and serve with chicken. Toothpicks can be used.

Serves 6 to 8 as an appetizer.

CHICKEN EN COQUILLES

Chicken in a shell is a lovely first course and couldn't be simpler to prepare.

>   3 cups chopped cooked chicken
>   ½ cup sherry
>   2 tablespoons butter
>   2 tablespoons flour
>   1 cup heavy cream
>   ¼ pound mushrooms, finely chopped
>   salt and pepper to taste
>   chopped parsley
>   ½ teaspoon paprika
>   1 tablespoon grated onion
>   1 garlic clove, crushed
>   bread crumbs
>   butter

Blend chicken with sherry, cover, and refrigerate for 1 hour. Melt butter, stir in flour, and cook for a minute or so. Add cream, chopped mushrooms, salt and pepper, parsley, paprika, onion, and garlic. Bring to a boil. Put mixture in individual shells, sprinkle with bread crumbs and dot with butter. Brown in preheated 350°F. oven until golden on top and bubbling.

Serves 6.

CHICKEN MOUSSE

1 pound chicken breasts, ground in food
    grinder (approximately 2½ to 3 cups)
3 egg yolks
6 tablespoons butter
½ cup bread crumbs
½ teaspoon Beau Monde seasoning
½ teaspoon tarragon
¼ teaspoon salt
    white pepper to taste
1½ cups heavy cream, whipped

Mix egg yolks with ground chicken. Cut butter into small pieces and stir into mixture. Add Beau Monde seasoning, tarragon, salt and white pepper. Whip cream and fold into mixture. Pack into mold and place in baking pan with enough water in pan to reach halfway up side of mold. Bake in preheated 350°F. oven for 45 minutes. Remove from oven and let stand a few minutes before unmolding.

This dish is especially good if allowed to cool and then refrigerate for several hours. It slices beautifully.

Serves 4 for luncheon dish or 6 to 8 as an appetizer.

CHICKEN RUMAKI

Rumaki is a fabulous appetizer usually made with chicken livers, but I think they are delicious when chicken is substituted.

2 chicken breasts, skinned, boned, and
    cut into 1-inch pieces
¾ cup sliced water chestnuts
½ pound sliced bacon, cut in half
    (should be at least 12 whole slices of
    bacon or use more)
toothpicks
½ cup soy sauce
3 tablespoons brown sugar
1 teaspoon fresh grated ginger, or ½ teaspoon
    ground ginger
1 clove garlic, crushed
4 tablespoons minced scallions
½ cup water

Make a small assembly line: a dish of chicken pieces; dish of sliced water chestnuts, plate with bacon, and toothpicks. Sandwich a piece of chicken and water chestnut together and wrap a piece of bacon around them. Secure with toothpick.

Make up as many Rumaki as there are pieces of bacon, at least 24. (Any leftover water chestnuts and chicken may be used for salad later.) In a large bowl combine soy sauce, brown sugar, ginger, garlic, scallions, and water. Stir until sugar is dissolved. Add Rumaki and gently toss so all are covered with marinade. Drain. Broil under medium heat until evenly browned and cooked. Turn several times to avoid burning.

Serves 4 to 6 as appetizer.

CHICKEN SATÉ

- 3 chicken breasts, skinned and boned
- 6 scallions, minced
- ½ cup soy sauce
- 2 tablespoons peanut oil
- 2 tablespoons dark corn syrup
- 1 teaspoon ground ginger
  juice of 1 lemon
- 1 tablespoon dry sherry
- 1 large onion, cut into 1-inch squares
- 1 large green pepper, cleaned and cut into
  1-inch squares

Cut chicken into 1-inch pieces. Mix scallions, soy sauce, peanut oil, corn syrup, ginger, lemon juice, and sherry in deep bowl. Marinate chicken for an hour or two.

Bring 1 quart of water to a boil and cook onion and green pepper squares for 3 minutes. Drain and cool. Thread 4 pieces of marinated chicken between squares of onion and pepper on small dampened wooden skewers. Grill under hot broiler, turning often until golden. Baste with marinade as you turn skewers. Should cook only 5 to 6 minutes all together.

Appetizers for 6 to 8 people.

CURRIED CHICKEN DIP

   2 large boiled chicken breasts
   1 3-ounce package cream cheese
   2 teaspoons curry powder
   2 tablespoons sesame seeds
   1 teaspoon soy sauce

Shred chicken breasts and put in mixing bowl. Add room-temperature cream cheese and mix vigorously. Add curry powder, sesame seeds, and soy sauce and blend thoroughly. Put into serving bowl and garnish with fresh chopped scallions or parsley. Serve with plain or onion crackers.

Appetizer for 8 to 10.

LUSCIOUS CHICKEN QUICHE

   1 9-inch uncooked pie shell
   2 tablespoons butter
   1 medium onion, finely minced
   ¾ cup grated Swiss cheese
   ½ cup cooked chicken, finely chopped
   ⅓ cup crisp crumbled bacon
   3 eggs
   1 cup light cream
   ¾ cup heavy cream
   1 tablespoon flour
      dash nutmeg
   ½ teaspoon salt

Melt butter in small skillet and sauté onion for 4 or 5 minutes until transparent. Cool slightly and sprinkle on uncooked pie shell with Swiss cheese, chopped chicken, and bacon. In a bowl combine eggs, light cream, heavy cream, flour, nutmeg, and salt. Pour over other ingredients in pie shell and bake in preheated oven at 375°F. for approximately 40 minutes.

Serves 6.

NUTTY CHICKEN SAILS

- 3 large chicken breasts, boned, skinned, and cut in half
- ¼ cup cornstarch
- 1 teaspoon salt
- 1 teaspoon sugar
- 2 egg whites
- 2 tablespoons sherry
- 1 teaspoon lemon juice
- ½ teaspoon grated orange rind
- 2 cups blanched almonds, ground or chopped fine
- 1 cup peanut or vegetable oil

Freeze boned and skinned chicken breasts because freezing makes them easier to slice. Then cut into slices ⅛ inch thick. Thaw. Combine cornstarch, salt, and sugar. Beat egg whites until fluffy, but not stiff, whisk in cornstarch mixture and add sherry, lemon juice, and grated orange rind. Dip chicken slices into egg white mixture and dredge in ground almonds. Fry in heated oil for 2 to 3 minutes on each side until golden. Drain. Cut slices into bite-size strips and thread on toothpicks. Serve on heated platter garnished with parsley or lemon slices.

Serves 8 as an appetizer.

CHICKEN
THE TRADITIONAL: BAKED

Baked chicken is often a family favorite—the dish everyone can agree upon. It is the adventuresome cook's favorite too—because the cook creates the flavor with imaginative ingredients and experimentation in this method of cooking. Baked chicken is moist and tender and usually easy to prepare. It is inexpensive, too. For that special economy meal a recipe that makes even chicken wings a delight is included.

BAKED ALMOND CHICKEN

8 serving pieces chicken
1 egg, beaten
1 tablespoon water
½ cup finely ground almonds
4 tablespoons butter, melted

Coat chicken with beaten egg and water mixture. Roll in ground almonds and place in buttered baking dish. Sprinkle melted butter over chicken. Bake in preheated 350°F. oven for 45 to 50 minutes.

Serves 4.

BAKED CHICKEN
WITH CHEESE AND ONIONS

1 3-pound chicken, cut into 8 serving pieces
    salt and pepper
4 tablespoons butter
2 tablespoons oil
2 large onions, sliced thin
1 cup grated Gruyère or Swiss cheese
4 tablespoons herbed bread crumbs
½ cup dry white wine
½ cup chicken stock

Season chicken with salt and pepper. Melt 2 tablespoons butter with oil in large skillet and brown chicken on all sides. Remove to side dish. Melt 2 remaining tablespoons butter in skillet and add sliced onions and cook, covered, until transparent, stirring occasionally. Place half of onions in shallow baking dish and arrange chicken on onions, then cover chicken with remaining onions. Mix grated cheese and bread crumbs and sprinkle over onions; pour wine and stock over top. Dot with butter. Place in preheated 350°F. oven for 45 to 50 minutes until golden on top.

Serves 4.

CHICKEN
AND POTATO LEEK BAKE

8 serving pieces chicken
2 tablespoons butter
1 tablespoon oil
1 package dried leek soup mix
2½ cups buttermilk
1 cup chicken broth
¼ pound fresh mushrooms, sliced
2 cups sliced potatoes

In ovenproof 4-quart casserole melt butter with oil and when hot brown chicken on all sides. Remove chicken to side dish as browned. In casserole put leek mix, buttermilk, and broth. Stir with whisk until powder of mix is dissolved. Then add mushrooms, potatoes, and chicken. Bake in preheated 350°F. oven for 45 to 50 minutes.

Serves 4.

CHICKEN ANITA

12 serving pieces of chicken
 2 garlic cloves
   salt and pepper
 4 tablespoons melted butter
 3 tablespoons flour
1½ cups boiling chicken broth
 ⅔ cup heated orange juice
 ¼ cup sherry
   grated peel of 1 lemon

Rub chicken with garlic cloves and season with salt and pepper. Place chicken in baking dish. Stir flour into melted butter, add boiling chicken broth, heated orange juice, sherry, and grated peel of lemon. Pour sauce over chicken. Bake in preheated 350°F. oven for 1 hour.

Serves 4 to 6.

CHICKEN BAKED IN CREAM

 8 serving pieces chicken
 4 or 5 tablespoons butter
 2 shallots, minced
   salt and pepper to taste
 2 cups light cream
 ¾ cup sherry

Melt butter in skillet and add shallots and sauté for 5 minutes. Remove to casserole. Season chicken, brown on all sides, and transfer to casserole. Pour cream and sherry over chicken. Bake in preheated 350°F. oven for 45 minutes. Remove chicken from casserole and whisk cream sauce for 5 minutes over heat on top of stove. Pour over chicken. Serve with herbed rice and green vegetables.

Serves 4 to 5.

CHICKEN BAKED IN SOUR CREAM

1 2½-to-3-pound chicken, cut into 8
      serving pieces
   salt and pepper
1 teaspoon paprika
3 teaspoons butter
2 tablespoons minced onion
1 cup sour cream
¼ cup milk

Season chicken with salt, pepper, and paprika. Brown in butter. Place in shallow baking dish and cover with combined onions, sour cream, and milk. Bake in preheated 350°F. oven for 35 minutes or until chicken is tender. If sour cream has thickened too much, add a little extra milk and stir with whisk before serving.

Serves 4.

CHICKEN BRAISED IN SHERRY

1 4-pound roasting chicken
4 tablespoons butter
1 tablespoon olive oil
1 carrot, chopped
1 medium onion, chopped
   pinch thyme
1 clove garlic, minced
1 bay leaf
   salt and pepper
1 cup dry sherry

In large ovenproof casserole brown chicken on all sides in butter and oil. Add remaining ingredients and bring to a boil. Baste chicken with butter and braise in covered casserole in 350°F. oven for 1 hour and 15 minutes. Baste every 15 to 20 minutes. Remove lid last 15 minutes of cooking. Transfer chicken to heated serving dish. Remove as much fat from juices in casserole as possible. Strain and pour over chicken.

Surround chicken with 1 pound sautéed whole fresh mushrooms.

Serves 4 to 5.

CHICKEN CHABLIS

    1 3-pound chicken, cut into 8 serving pieces
    4 tablespoons butter
    3 tablespoons oil
   16 small white onions
   ¼ pound fresh mushrooms, quartered
    4 shallots, minced
    2 garlic cloves, minced
    1 cup Chablis
   ½ cup heavy cream
      fresh chopped parsley

In skillet melt 3 tablespoons butter with 2 tablespoons oil and brown seasoned chicken on all sides.
Transfer chicken to ovenproof casserole. Add remaining 1 tablespoon butter and 1 tablespoon oil to skillet
and quickly brown onions, shaking pan often. Remove
onions with slotted spoon and add to casserole. Sauté
mushrooms, shallots, and garlic for 5 minutes, then
transfer to casserole. Pour wine in skillet and scrape
bottom of pan to release any particles sticking there.
Bring to a boil. Pour into casserole, cover, and cook in
preheated 350°F. oven for 40 minutes. Remove
chicken, onions, and mushrooms to heated serving dish
and keep warm. Bring liquid in casserole to a boil on
top of the stove and reduce by half. Pour cream into
casserole and heat until sauce thickens slightly. Check
seasoning and pour sauce over chicken. Garnish with
fresh chopped parsley.

Serves 4.

CHICKEN GINGER

- 1 3-pound chicken, cut into 8 serving pieces
  salt and pepper
- 1 cup plain yoghurt
- 2 teaspoons ground ginger
- ½ teaspoon Kitchen Bouquet
- ¼ cup heavy cream

Season chicken with salt and pepper. Place in a bowl and add yoghurt blended with Kitchen Bouquet and ginger. Coat each piece thoroughly, cover, and refrigerate overnight. Place chicken and sauce in casserole and bake in preheated 500°F. oven for 15 minutes. Reduce heat to 350°F. and cook 30 minutes longer. Take chicken out of casserole, add heavy cream, and stir briskly with whisk. Adjust seasoning with ginger and/or salt. Return chicken and serve. Accompany with frozen green peas, cooked in 3 tablespoons butter with salt and pepper, and crusty French bread.

Serves 4.

CHICKEN VAN DAMM

8 serving pieces chicken
3 tablespoons melted butter
3 ounces cream cheese
1 teaspoon powdered rosemary
½ teaspoon salt
  pepper to taste
1 teaspoon paprika
  juice of 1 lemon

Arrange pieces of chicken in greased shallow baking dish, skin side up. Mix butter, cream cheese, rosemary, salt, pepper, and paprika together and spread mixture on each piece of chicken. Sprinkle with lemon juice and roast in preheated 375°F. oven for 15 minutes. Reduce heat to 350°F. and cook 25 to 35 minutes more or until tender.

Serves 4.

CHICKEN VERONIQUE

- 2 tablespoons butter
- 2 tablespoons oil
- 1 3-pound chicken, cut into 8 serving pieces
  salt and pepper
- ½ teaspoon tarragon
- 1½ tablespoons minced onion
- 2 cups seedless white grapes
- ½ cup dry white wine
- ½ cup chicken broth
- 1 tablespoon cornstarch
- ¼ cup heavy cream

Melt butter with oil in ovenproof casserole on top of stove. Brown seasoned chicken quickly. Add tarragon, onion, grapes, white wine, and broth. Cover and bake in preheated 375°F. oven for 35 minutes. Remove lid and cook 5 minutes longer. Transfer chicken to heated serving dish and cover to keep warm. Whisk cornstarch dissolved in a little water into sauce. Add cream. Stir constantly and cook for 3 or 4 minutes until sauce thickens slightly. Pour over chicken.

Serves 4.

CHICKEN WINGS LOUISE

Here's an economical dish and one that those who love to eat with their fingers will enjoy.

- 12 large chicken wings, wing tips removed
- 3 tablespoons olive oil
- 3 tablespoons lemon juice
- 1 clove garlic, crushed
- ½ teaspoon dried tarragon
- 1 bay leaf
-    salt and pepper to taste
- 2 tablespoons butter

In a large bowl combine oil, lemon juice, garlic, tarragon, bay leaf, salt and pepper. Coat wings with mixture, cover, and refrigerate overnight. Place chicken wings in baking dish and dot with butter. Bake in preheated 400°F. oven for 15 minutes. Turn chicken wings and cook 15 to 20 minutes more until chicken is golden. Serve with plain or curried rice.

Serves 4.

FOIL-BAKED
BARBEQUE CHICKEN

   1 3-pound chicken, cut into 8 serving pieces
  ⅔ cup ketchup
  ⅓ cup wine vinegar
  2 teaspoons prepared mustard
  1 teaspoon paprika
  2 tablespoons melted butter
  1 tablespoon Worcestershire sauce
  2 cloves garlic, crushed
  ½ teaspoon oregano
  ½ teaspoon chili powder
  ¼ teaspoon sugar
  1 teaspoon salt
  1 cup sliced onions

Combine all ingredients except onions and chicken and bring to a boil. Remove from heat. Line a shallow baking dish with buttered foil and arrange chicken and onions on foil. Pour sauce over chicken then cover with another large sheet of foil. Bake in preheated 375°F. oven for 40 minutes. Remove top sheet of foil and bake 10 minutes more.

Serves 4.

MUSTARD-COATED CHICKEN

- 8 serving pieces chicken
- 2 tablespoons bread crumbs
- 3 tablespoons Dijon mustard
- 2 tablespoons vegetable oil
- ¼ cup chicken broth
- ¼ teaspoon salt
  pepper to taste

Mix together bread crumbs, mustard, vegetable oil, broth, and salt and pepper. Coat chicken in mixture and place in well-greased baking dish. Cook in preheated 350°F. oven for 45 minutes or until chicken is tender.

Serves 4.

POËLE POULET

- 1 3-to-3½-pound chicken
- 3 tablespoons butter
- 1 large onion, chopped
- 1 stalk celery with leaves, chopped
- 2 carrots, chopped
- 1 stick butter or 4 ounces
  bouquet garni made of 1 bay leaf,
      3 sprigs parsley, ½ teaspoon thyme,
      and 6 peppercorns

Melt 3 tablespoons butter in bottom of heavy casserole and sauté onions, celery, and carrots for 5 minutes. Put 1 stick of butter inside chicken, sew up, and truss. Put chicken on top of vegetables, and add bouquet garni. Cover and place in preheated 350°F. oven. Immediately turn oven down to 300°F. and cook for 1½ hours, basting frequently. Remove cover and continue cooking for 30 minutes more. Transfer chicken to heated serving platter. Strain liquid left in casserole, carefully pressing vegetables with spoon to squeeze out as much of their juices as possible. Serve juice in sauceboat.

Serves 4.

POULET VICHY

  1 3-pound chicken, cut into 8 serving pieces
  4 tablespoons butter
  3 tablespoons sherry
  2 carrots, chopped
  2 medium onions, sliced
  6 mushrooms, sliced
    salt and pepper
  1 tablespoon flour
  1 cup chicken stock
  ½ cup red wine
  1 tablespoon tomato paste
  1 bay leaf
  6 large carrots, scraped and sliced thin
  ½ cup white wine
  2 tablespoons lemon juice
  3 tablespoons heavy cream
  1 tablespoon chopped parsley

Melt 2 tablespoons butter in bottom of ovenproof casserole and brown chicken on all sides. Pour in sherry and ignite. Remove chicken and add chopped carrots, onions, and mushrooms. Season with salt and pepper and sprinkle flour over mixture. Stir and add 1 cup chicken stock. Replace chicken, add red wine and tomato paste. Bring to a boil, add bay leaf, cover, and cook in 350°F. oven for 40 minutes. Meanwhile, melt 2 tablespoons of remaining butter in pan, add white wine, lemon juice, 3 tablespoons water and 6 sliced carrots. Season, cover, and cook slowly until tender, about 15 to 18 minutes. Remove from heat and add cream and parsley. When chicken is done transfer to heated serving dish. Strain juices left in pan and pour over chicken. Divide carrots in half and place at each end of dish.

Serves 4.

SAUCY CHICKEN WITH CHERRIES

   1 3½-pound chicken, cut into serving pieces
     salt and pepper
   1 garlic clove, crushed
   2 tablespoons butter
   2 tablespoons oil
   ½ cup chicken broth
   ½ cup orange juice
   1 tablespoon lemon juice
   2 teaspoons Worcestershire sauce
   ¼ cup brown sugar
   ¼ cup raisins
   ¼ cup port
   1½ cups canned pitted sour cherries
   1 tablespoon cornstarch

Season chicken with salt and pepper. Melt butter with oil and add garlic. Push garlic around in the pan for a minute and brown chicken on all sides. Meanwhile, blend a sauce from remaining ingredients except for cherries and cornstarch. Place chicken in casserole and pour sauce over chicken. Cover and bake in preheated 350°F. oven for 35 minutes. Add cherries, blend in, and bake 10 minutes longer, uncovered. Transfer chicken to heated serving dish and add cornstarch, which has been dissolved in a little water. Bring to a boil on top of stove and when sauce thickens, pour over chicken and serve immediately.

Serves 4.

CHICKEN
THE TRADITIONAL: BREAST

Boned chicken breasts are sold prepackaged in many markets and if saving time is a factor then by all means buy them. But the cost is quite a bit more when purchased that way and boning is not difficult. Split the breast in half. Pull off skin with fingers. It comes off easily. Insert a small knife between the meat and breastbone and, using knife and fingers, work flesh away from bone or bones. Be careful not to tear flesh. Repeat on other breast half. Trim pieces.

Some recipes call for the chicken breast to be flattened. To do this, place the breast between two pieces of waxed paper and gently beat with a rolling pin or the side of a meat cleaver. Try not to break the flesh.

BREASTS OF CHICKEN
ALEXANDRA

2 large chicken breasts, skinned, boned,
    and cut in half
  salt and white pepper
2 tablespoons butter
1 tablespoon oil
1 cup heavy cream
1 package frozen French-style green beans
4 slices fried French bread, 1 inch thick
1 tablespoon flour
3 tablespoons dry white wine or vermouth or
    chicken broth
3 tablespoons grated Swiss cheese
  paprika

Season chicken with salt and pepper. Melt butter
with oil and brown chicken on both sides. Add ½ cup
of cream and bring to a boil. Immediately lower heat
and simmer for 10 minutes. Meanwhile, cook green
beans according to package directions. Place drained
cooked green beans in equal portions on slices of fried
bread in ovenproof serving dish. Top each with piece
of chicken. Cover and place in warm oven while
finishing sauce. Add remaining ½ cup of cream to
cream in pan. Bring to a boil and reduce heat. Mix
flour with dry white wine (or vermouth, or chicken
broth) and whisk into cream. Then add cheese, whisking constantly until cheese melts and sauce thickens
slightly. Season well with salt and pepper. Pour over
each chicken breast. Sprinkle with paprika and place
under hot broiler for a few minutes until sauce is
golden.

Serves 4.

CHICKEN AND GREEN PEPPERS

2 whole chicken breasts
3 tablespoons peanut or vegetable oil
3 medium green peppers, cleaned and cut
   into 1-inch pieces
1 or 2 garlic cloves, minced
½ teaspoon sugar
1 tablespoon soy sauce
½ teaspoon ground ginger
2 cups chicken stock
2 tablespoons cornstarch

Boil chicken breasts in water to cover for 20 minutes. Strain off stock and reserve 2 cups. Remove skin and bones from chicken breasts and cut into bite-sized pieces. Heat oil and sauté green peppers and garlic for 5 minutes over medium high heat. Reduce heat, add chicken, sugar, soy sauce, ginger, salt and pepper to taste, and the chicken stock that was set aside. Bring to a boil and add cornstarch that has been dissolved in a little water. Reduce heat under chicken to a simmer and cook, covered, for 10 minutes. Adjust seasoning. Serve on fluffy white rice.

Serves 4.

CHICKEN BREASTS AU GRATIN

    4 chicken breasts, skinned, boned, and halved
    2 leeks, finely sliced
    1 tablespoon fresh chopped parsley
    ⅛ teaspoon dried thyme
    ½ cup dry white wine
    ½ cup chicken stock
      salt and pepper to taste
    1 cup grated Swiss cheese
    2 tablespoons dried bread crumbs

In large buttered shallow baking dish place chicken, finely sliced leeks, parsley, and thyme. Pour white wine and chicken stock over chicken. Season with salt and pepper. Cover with piece of buttered foil and place in preheated 375°F. oven for 25 minutes. Remove foil and sprinkle combined cheese and bread crumbs over chicken. Broil until cheese turns golden.

Serves 4 to 6.

CHICKEN BREASTS IN MARSALA

- 4 chicken breasts, halved
- salt and pepper
- 2 tablespoons butter
- 4 tablespoons olive oil
- ½ cup chicken stock
- ½ cup Marsala wine
- ¼ pound mushrooms, sliced
- fresh chopped parsley

In large ovenproof casserole melt butter with olive oil and brown seasoned chicken breasts a few at a time. Pour off all but 1 tablespoon fat. Add chicken stock and Marsala. Cover and simmer for 30 minutes. Add mushrooms, cover, and cook 5 minutes longer. Garnish with fresh chopped parsley.

Serves 4 to 6.

CHICKEN BREASTS IN PORT

4 chicken breasts, skinned, boned, and halved
1 medium onion, chopped
1 carrot, chopped
1 stalk celery, chopped
1 bay leaf
3 sprigs parsley
1 quart chicken stock
5 tablespoons butter
2 tablespoons flour
1 cup mushrooms, sliced
¼ cup port
½ cup heavy cream
   salt and pepper
   fresh chopped parsley

Put chicken, onion, carrot, celery, bay leaf, parsley, and chicken stock in Dutch oven and bring to a boil. Reduce heat and simmer for 35 minutes. Meanwhile, melt 2 tablespoons butter in skillet and sauté sliced mushrooms for 5 minutes. Remove chicken breasts, keep warm, and strain stock. Melt 3 remaining tablespoons of butter in saucepan, stir in flour, and cook a few minutes. Slowly pour in 1 cup of strained stock, stirring constantly. Add mushrooms, port, and heavy cream. Adjust seasoning. Heat thoroughly and pour over chicken. Garnish with chopped parsley.

Serves 4 to 6.

CHICKEN BREASTS IN RICH MUSHROOM SAUCE

4 chicken breasts, halved
salt and pepper
1 stick butter
1 medium onion, chopped
½ pound fresh mushrooms, sliced
1½ cups heavy cream
⅓ cup sherry
fresh chopped parsley

Pat chicken dry with paper towels and season with salt and pepper. Melt ½ stick butter in large skillet and brown chicken on skin side only a few pieces at a time. Remove chicken and add remaining butter, onion, and mushrooms. Cook for 5 minutes over medium heat. Add cream and sherry. Bring to a boil, then reduce heat to a simmer. Return chicken to pan and coat with mushroom sauce. Cover and simmer for 25 minutes. Transfer chicken to heated serving dish and pour sauce over chicken. Garnish with fresh chopped parsley.

Serves 4 to 6.

CHICKEN BREASTS
WITH PARMESAN

4 chicken breasts, skinned, boned, and halved
2 eggs, beaten
1½ cups grated Parmesan cheese
1 stick butter or 8 tablespoons
1 cup mushrooms, finely minced
1 tablespoon fresh chopped parsley
2 tablespoons dry white wine

Season chicken with salt and pepper. Dip each piece in beaten eggs and roll in Parmesan cheese, then refrigerate for 30 minutes. Heat 4 tablespoons butter and sauté pieces of chicken, a few at a time, until golden on both sides. Add butter as needed. Transfer chicken to heated serving dish when finished. With at least 2 tablespoons butter in pan, sauté mushrooms and parsley over high heat for 3 or 4 minutes, pour in wine, and bring to a boil. Pour over chicken.

Serves 4.

CHICKEN CORDON BLEU

2 large chicken breasts, skinned, boned,
   and halved
8 tablespoons butter
4 shallots, minced
3 tablespoons dry white wine
2 tablespoons dried bread crumbs
   salt and pepper
4 slices Swiss cheese
4 thin slices ham, regular or prosciutto
1 tablespoon lemon juice
   bread crumbs for dredging

Sauté shallots in 3 tablespoons butter for 5 minutes.
Pour in dry white wine and stir in 2 tablespoons bread
crumbs. Remove from heat. Place chicken breast
halves between two pieces of wax paper and pound to
flatten. Sprinkle with salt and pepper. Spread shallot
mixture evenly on pieces of chicken. Top each with
slice of cheese and ham. Roll up chicken and secure
with toothpicks or string. Melt 5 tablespoons remaining butter and blend with lemon juice. Roll chicken in
butter mixture and dredge in bread crumbs. Place in
buttered baking dish and bake in preheated 350°F.
oven for 35 to 40 minutes.

Serves 4.

CHICKEN IN CREAM SAUCE

3 chicken breasts, cut into thin strips
4 tablespoons butter
2 tablespoons vegetable oil
4 shallots, chopped
½ cup mushrooms, chopped
⅓ cup dry white wine
1 cup heavy cream
dash nutmeg
salt and white pepper to taste

Melt 2 tablespoons of butter in skillet and add oil. Add ½ chicken strips and toss with fork until golden. Remove cooked chicken strips to side dish. Add 2 more tablespoons of butter and rest of chicken strips to skillet and cook as before. When the rest of the chicken has been removed to the side dish, add shallots and mushrooms to skillet. Add more butter if needed. Cook for 3 or 4 minutes, pour in wine, and bring to a boil. Add cream and simmer for 10 minutes, stirring often. Season with nutmeg, salt and pepper. Return chicken to pan for a few minutes until chicken is thoroughly heated.

Serves 4.

Serve with curried rice, garnish with pimiento or fresh chopped parsley.

CHICKEN SUPREMES WITH
FOIE GRAS SAUCE

- 3 large chicken breasts, skinned, boned, and halved
- 4 tablespoons butter
- 1 tablespoon oil
- ½ cup foie gras
- ½ cup heavy cream
- 2 tablespoons brandy
- salt and pepper

Melt butter in large skillet and add oil. Gently sauté chicken breasts until lightly golden on both sides. Meanwhile, mix together foie gras and heavy cream. Season with salt and pepper and set aside. When chicken has cooked, transfer to heated serving dish. Pour brandy in skillet, heat, and (standing well back) ignite. When flame goes out, add foie gras mixture and whisk until smooth. Pour over chicken.

Serves 4.

CHICKEN SUPREMES WITH MOZZARELLA

4 chicken breasts, skinned, boned, and halved
3 tablespoons butter
2 tablespoons oil
8 mushrooms, sliced
8 thin slices mozzarella cheese
½ cup dry white wine
½ cup chicken stock
2 tablespoons brandy

Melt 2 tablespoons butter with 2 tablespoons oil and brown chicken breasts quickly on each side. Add more butter and oil in equal amounts if needed. Transfer browned breasts to shallow baking dish. Place 1 sliced mushroom on each piece of chicken and cover with a slice of mozzarella cheese. Pour wine, stock, and brandy into skillet in which chicken was browned. Bring to a boil, scraping up any particles remaining on bottom and sides of pan. Swirl in remaining table- spoon of butter, then pour into baking dish with chicken. Place in hot oven under broiler until cheese is golden.

Serves 4.

CHICKEN WITH SESAME SEEDS AND BROCCOLI

2 large chicken breasts, skinned, boned, and
    cut into 2-inch strips
8 slices bacon
2 tablespoons butter
1 garlic clove, mashed
4 scallions, sliced
2 packages frozen broccoli spears, thawed
    and cut into thirds
1 tablespoon soy sauce
1 tablespoon sherry
1 cup chicken broth
1 tablespoon cornstarch
2 tablespoons sesame seeds, toasted

In large skillet fry bacon until crisp and drain on absorbent paper. Remove all but 1 tablespoon bacon drippings and add butter. When heated, add garlic and scallions. Push around in skillet for a minute. Add chicken and cook until slightly golden. Add broccoli, soy sauce, and sherry. Cover and simmer for 5 minutes. Add stock and cornstarch that has been dissolved with a little water. Gently stir. Cook for 5 minutes longer and remove to heated serving dish and garnish with crumbled bacon and toasted sesame seeds.

Serves 4.

CHICKEN WITH SNOW PEA PODS

1½ pounds chicken breasts, skinned, boned,
and cut into thin strips
5 tablespoons peanut oil or vegetable oil
1 garlic clove, minced
1 medium onion, sliced thin
½ teaspoon ginger
1 package frozen snow pea pods, thawed
1 cup bamboo shoots, sliced
½ cup water chestnuts, sliced thin
2 tablespoons soy sauce
1 tablespoon sherry
½ teaspoon sugar
¼ teaspoon MSG (optional)
1 tablespoon cornstarch

Heat 3 tablespoons oil in skillet and sauté garlic, onion, and ginger for 5 minutes. Add chicken strips and fry for 5 minutes very briskly. Transfer to side dish. Add 2 tablespoons oil to skillet and fry snow peas, bamboo shoots, and water chestnuts for 3 minutes. In bowl mix together soy sauce, sherry, sugar, and MSG if used. Pour into vegetables and bring to a quick boil over high heat, reduce heat, and add chicken. Simmer a few minutes. Meanwhile, dissolve cornstarch with a little water and add to mixture, stirring constantly until sauce thickens slightly. Serve on rice.

Serves 4.

CRAB-STUFFED CHICKEN BREASTS

4 chicken breasts, skinned, boned, and halved
1 medium onion, chopped
1 stalk celery, minced
5 tablespoons butter
½ cup dry white wine
6 ounces crab meat, flaked
6 black olives, finely chopped
½ cup seasoned bread crumbs
¼ teaspoon salt
  pepper to taste
½ cup chicken stock

Melt 3 tablespoons butter in skillet and sauté onion and celery for 5 minutes until transparent. Remove from heat and add ¼ cup wine, crab meat, chopped olives, bread crumbs, and salt and pepper to taste. Combine. Place chicken pieces between two pieces of wax paper and flatten slightly. Place equal amount of filling mixture in middle of breast halves. Roll up, securing with string or toothpick, and put in baking dish. Pour remaining wine and broth in baking dish. Dot chicken with 2 tablespoons butter. Bake in preheated 350°F. oven for 45 to 50 minutes until chicken is tender and golden on top.

Serves 4 to 6.

CREAMY CHICKEN CURRY

*Here is an excellent easy dish particularly good for a
buffet dinner.*

4 chicken breasts, skinned, boned, and
cut into bite-sized strips
salt and white pepper
2 tablespoons curry powder
3 tablespoons butter
1 tablespoon oil
1 garlic clove, crushed
½ cup minced shallots
3 cups chicken stock
2 tablespoons flour
1 cup heavy cream
fresh chopped parsley
1 cup toasted almond slivers

Season chicken with salt, white pepper, and curry
powder. Melt butter in large skillet with oil and sauté
chicken with garlic and shallots until lightly brown.
Pour in chicken stock and bring to a boil. Cover and
simmer for ½ hour. Mix flour with enough chicken
stock to make smooth paste. Add to chicken with heavy
cream, stirring constantly. When sauce thickens slightly
and is thoroughly heated, adjust seasoning. Place in
chafing dish and sprinkle with fresh chopped parsley
and toasted almond slivers. Serve with fluffy white
rice and a side dish of chutney.

Serves 6.

LEMON CHICKEN AND
CRAB MEAT

2 large chicken breasts, boned, skinned, and
   cut into thin 2-inch strips
3 tablespoons butter
3 tablespoons vegetable oil
8 scallions, sliced
   flour
1½ cups chicken broth
   juice of 2 lemons
1 package frozen artichoke hearts (thawed)
1 pound package frozen crab meat (thawed)
1 small can water chestnuts, drained and sliced
2 tablespoons cornstarch
1 tablespoon soy sauce
   freshly ground pepper to taste

Put 1½ tablespoons each of butter and oil in skillet.
Add scallions and cook for 5 minutes, stirring occasionally. Remove scallions to side dish leaving as much
of butter and oil as possible in pan. Add remaining
butter and oil. Heat. Toss chicken slices in flour and
shake off extra flour. Sauté chicken over medium heat,
stirring frequently, until golden. Transfer to side dish
with scallions. Add chicken broth and the juice of two
lemons to skillet. Scrape bottom of skillet with wooden
spoon. Bring broth to a boil, add chicken, artichoke
hearts and simmer for 8 minutes. Add crab meat,
scallions, water chestnuts, soy sauce, and pepper to
taste. Stir gently. Cook for 5 minutes. Dissolve cornstarch in a little water and stir into mixture. When
sauce thickens serve immediately.

Serves 4 to 6.

MAUREEN'S SUPREME CHICKEN PIE

        2 large chicken breasts
        1 bay leaf
        1 medium onion, cut in half
        1 carrot, chopped
        ½ teaspoon salt
          pepper to taste
        3 tablespoons butter
        4 tablespoons flour
      1½ cups chicken stock
        3 tablespoons white wine or dry vermouth
        1 6-ounce can water chestnuts, sliced
        1 large carrot, scraped and grated
        ½ teaspoon dried tarragon
        ¼ teaspoon Lawry's Seasoned Salt
          9-inch double piecrust

Place chicken breasts in saucepan with bay leaf, onion, chopped carrot, salt and pepper to taste. Cover with cold water and bring to a boil. Reduce heat to a simmer and cook, covered, for 30 minutes or until meat comes off the bone easily. Transfer chicken to plate and cool. Strain stock and reserve 1½ cups for use later in recipe. In clean saucepan melt butter and stir in flour. Cook over low heat for a minute, stirring constantly. Slowly pour in stock, always whisking. Add wine. Consistency should be fairly thick. Set sauce aside. Remove skin from chicken breasts and bone. Shred chicken breasts and add to sauce with sliced water chestnuts, grated carrot, tarragon, Lawry's Seasoned Salt, and pepper. Combine mixture and taste for seasoning. Line a 9-inch pie plate with piecrust and fill with chicken mixture. Cut a small hole in the

center of piecrust top and cover pie with crust. Crimp
edges and bake in preheated 375°F. oven for 30 to
35 minutes until pie crust is golden brown.

Serves 4.

This dish may be served hot or cold.

PETTI DI
POLLO ALLA BOLOGNESE
(*Chicken Breasts, Prosciutto, and Cheese*)

> 2 large chicken breasts, skinned, boned, and
>   cut in half—flattened slightly
>   salt and pepper
>   flour for dredging
> 1 stick butter or 4 ounces
> 1 teaspoon oregano
> ⅓ pound prosciutto or Virginia ham
> ½ pound Bel Paese cheese, cut into thin slices
> 3 or 4 tablespoons grated Parmesan cheese
> ⅔ cup chicken stock

Place each chicken breast half between pieces of
wax paper and pound gently to flatten. Discard wax
paper and trim pieces of chicken to approximately the
same size. Season with salt and pepper and dredge in
flour. Melt 4 tablespoons butter in large skillet. When
butter foaming subsides, add breasts and sauté until
golden, about 3 or 4 minutes on each side. Put browned
breasts in buttered baking dish. Sprinkle lightly with
oregano and top with a slice of prosciutto and Bel

Paese. Add chicken stock and sprinkle grated Parmesan cheese over each piece of chicken. Place in preheated 350°F. oven and bake for 10 to 12 minutes, then put under broiler for a minute or two until cheese is golden brown.

Serves 4.

RUPERT'S CHICKEN SUPREME

  2 large chicken breasts, skinned, boned, and halved
  4 slices white bread
    oil for deep-fat frying
    salt and pepper to taste
  6 tablespoons butter
  8 ounces egg noodles
  ¼ cup heavy cream
  2 tablespoons white wine
  2 tablespoons Parmesan cheese
  1 tablespoon dried bread crumbs

MORNAY SAUCE

  2 tablespoons butter
  2 tablespoons flour
  1½ cups milk
  ¾ cup cheddar cheese

With heart-shaped cookie cutter, cut heart out of each slice of white bread and fry in oil until golden. Drain on absorbent paper. Season chicken with salt and pepper to taste. Melt 3 tablespoons butter in skillet and brown chicken pieces on each side. Set aside and cover to keep warm. Cook egg noodles according to package directions. While they are cooking prepare Mornay Sauce by melting 2 tablespoons butter in saucepan; stir in flour and cook over low heat, stirring, for a minute. Slowly pour in milk, whisking constantly. Season with salt and pepper to taste and add cheese, stirring until it melts. Set aside and put piece of foil down on top of sauce to prevent skin from forming. When noodles are cooked, immediately drain and toss with 3 tablespoons butter, heavy cream, and white wine. Season with salt and pepper to taste and arrange on bottom of baking dish; top with pieces of chicken, then pour Mornay Sauce evenly over chicken. Combine Parmesan cheese with bread crumbs and sprinkle over sauce. Place under preheated broiler until golden brown. Garnish dish with heart-shaped croûtes.

Serves 4.

SAUTEED CHICKEN BREASTS MARSALA

4 chicken breasts, skinned and boned
   salt and pepper
2 tablespoons butter
2 tablespoons olive oil
½ cup Marsala
½ cup chicken broth
¼ pound mushrooms, sliced
¼ cup heavy cream
   fresh chopped parsley

Split breasts in half and season with salt and pepper. Brown on both sides in melted butter with olive oil, a few pieces at a time. Remove to side dish as browned. Add Marsala and chicken broth to pan. Bring to a rapid boil. Place chicken in pan along with mushrooms and simmer for 10 minutes. Place chicken in heated serving dish. Add cream to pan, bring to a boil, and stir vigorously for 1 minute. Adjust seasoning. Pour sauce over chicken and garnish with fresh chopped parsley.

Serves 4.

CHICKEN THE TRADITIONAL: BROILED AND GRILLED

Chicken lends itself beautifully to broiling and grilling. Keep the bird well basted and cook evenly by turning. If time permits marinate the chicken overnight or for a few hours. Several seasonings and herbs are especially suitable for use with this cooking method: Beau Monde seasoning, Lawry's Seasoned Salt, paprika, tarragon, or rosemary.

BROILED CHICKEN WITH COCONUT MILK

    1 2½-pound broiling chicken
    2 cups coconut milk*
    1 teaspoon turmeric
    1 medium onion, chopped
    ¼ teaspoon salt
      melted butter for basting

Place chicken in a large pot and add coconut milk, turmeric, onion, and salt. Bring to a boil and simmer about 15 to 20 minutes. Transfer chicken to oven, baste a little on each side with coconut-stock and butter, and broil until golden.

Serves 4.

* Soak 1 cup shredded coconut in 2 cups milk for several hours in the refrigerator. Drain and squeeze out extra juice from coconut through cloth.

BROILED CHICKEN WITH LEMON, BUTTER, AND GARLIC

1 2½-pound broiling chicken, cut into 8
   serving pieces
⅓ cup freshly squeezed lemon juice
1 clove garlic, crushed
1 stick butter or ¼ pound
2 teaspoons oregano
   salt and pepper to taste

Wash chicken and pat dry with paper towels. In deep bowl mix lemon juice, melted butter, garlic, oregano, and salt and pepper to taste. Dip chicken in mixture and place chicken on broiler rack, 6 to 8 inches from flame, and broil for 15 minutes, or until lightly browned. Turn each piece of chicken and baste with lemon mixture and broil 10 minutes longer or until tender and nicely browned.

Serves 4.

CHICKEN BROCHETTES

16 1½-inch pieces raw chicken
16 1-inch slices bacon
16 mushroom caps
 2 eggs, beaten
   bread crumbs

Thread alternate pieces of chicken, bacon, and mushroom caps on metal skewers. Four pieces of each should be on every skewer. Roll each skewer in beaten eggs and then coat in bread crumbs. Grill under hot broiler until evenly cooked and golden.

Serves 2 to 4.

CHICKEN
GINGER SHISH KABOBS

- 4 whole chicken breasts, skinned, boned, and cut into 1½-inch pieces
- 2 tablespoons butter
- 2 tablespoons oil
- 8 shallots, chopped
- 1 large yellow onion, cut in half and quartered
- 2 medium-sized zucchini, sliced ⅓ inch thick
- 2 medium-sized yellow squash, sliced ⅓ inch thick
- 1 cup honey
- ½ cup soy sauce
- 1 teaspoon grated ginger root or ½ teaspoon ground ginger

Heat butter and oil in skillet. Add shallots and sauté until transparent. Remove with slotted spoon and place in bowl and save for marinade. Sauté pieces of chicken just until the chicken turns white. Prepare each kabob in the following way: slice of onion, piece of chicken, slice of zucchini, slice of onion, chicken, and yellow squash. Repeat until 4 pieces of chicken are on each kabob ending with a slice of onion. Prepare 8 skewers and place in large shallow dish. Mix shallots, honey, soy sauce, and ginger. Pour over kabobs and marinate for about 1 hour, turning once. Broil for a few minutes on each side until golden, basting when turned.

Serves 4.

CHICKEN LIVER BROCHETTES

    8 chicken livers
    8 slices bacon
   16 inch-square pieces of onion
      Lawry's Seasoned Salt

Drop onion squares into boiling water and boil for 2 minutes. Drain. Cut chicken livers and bacon slices in half. Alternate slice of onion, piece of chicken liver, and rolled up bacon on skewers until 4 pieces of each are on each of 4 skewers. Sprinkle lightly with Lawry's Seasoned Salt. Place under hot broiler, about 6 inches from flame. Cook and turn until done.

Careful not to burn.

Serves 2.

CHICKEN TERIYAKI

Teriyaki is a Hawaiian dish of beef strips marinated in a tangy sauce. It is surprisingly good made with strips of chicken.

> 2 pounds chicken breasts, skinned, boned, and halved, cut into strips 3 or 4 inches long and 1 inch thick
> 1 clove garlic, crushed
> 1 tablespoon fresh minced ginger or 1 teaspoon ground ginger
> 2 tablespoons sugar
> 1 medium onion, chopped
> 1 cup soy sauce
> ½ cup sherry
> ¼ cup water

Place chicken strips in bowl. Mix together remaining ingredients and pour over chicken. Cover and marinate for 2 or 3 hours. Remove chicken and thread on 6-inch steel or dampened wooden skewers. Broil under preheated broiler. Watch carefully. Cook about 3 or 4 minutes on each side, until golden. Baste with marinade when turning skewers. Serve on rice.

Serves 4.

This dish is also an excellent appetizer for 8.

HAPPY CHICKEN

- 1 chicken breast, cut in half
- 3 chicken thighs
- 3 chicken legs
- 1 bottle Russian dressing (8 ounces)
- ¾ cup apricot preserves
- 2 tablespoons lemon juice
- 1 teaspoon ground ginger
- 2 tablespoons scallions, minced
- 1 teaspoon salt
  freshly ground pepper

Place chicken in shallow dish. Mix remaining ingredients together and pour over chicken. Marinate for several hours—turning occasionally. Broil 8 inches below broiler, turning and basting with marinade every 8 minutes for about 24 minutes or until tender and golden. Watch carefully not to burn.

Serves 4.

LEMON AND TARRAGON GRILLED CHICKEN

2 broilers about 2 pounds each—halved,
    backbones removed
  salt and pepper
½ stick butter or 4 tablespoons
1 tablespoon lemon juice
2 teaspoons tarragon

Season chicken with salt and pepper. Melt butter and add lemon juice and tarragon. Brush generously on chicken and grill skin side down on the grill. Turn a few times and continue basting until done.

Serves 4.

PINEAPPLE BROILED CHICKEN

2 2-pound broiling chickens—split in half
    with backbone removed
  salt and pepper
1 teaspoon ground ginger
2 teaspoons brown sugar
2 tablespoons melted butter
2 tablespoons lemon juice
½ cup canned crushed pineapple, reserve juice

Wash and pat chicken dry. Season with salt and pepper. Mix pineapple juice, ginger, brown sugar, melted butter, and lemon juice in small bowl. Baste chicken bone side up with mixture and broil for about 10 minutes. Turn and baste skin side of chicken and broil for 8 minutes. Spread about 2 tablespoons crushed pineapple on each chicken half and broil until pineapple and chicken are golden brown.

Serves 4.

CHICKEN THE TRADITIONAL: FRIED

Fried chicken is an American tradition and each section of the country has its special way of preparing it. Fried chicken brings with it a lot of pleasant memories: the picnic table, Sunday's big family dinner, a packed lunch box for a long trip, father's favorite piece that no one touches. Methods of frying are varied and often dictated by local custom: deep-fat fried, oven-fried, smothered in gravy, sautéed in butter and herbs, or coated in batter. It's been fun gathering these fried chicken recipes from restaurants, friends, and neighbors—each of whom is sure his method is best.

CHICKEN BITTNER

This recipe is named in honor of its originator, Jack Bittner, an actor with an excellent bass voice. He is also a fine cook. In East Haddam, Connecticut, where we worked together in summer stock, we could buy beautiful fresh-killed chickens at a nearby farm. One day, while I watched, he prepared this simple but delicious chicken. We were soon joined by a host of hungry actors who wanted to know what was on the stove.

- 8 serving pieces chicken
- 8 tablespoons butter
- ½ teaspoon garlic powder
- ½ teaspoon dried minced onion
- 1 teaspoon salt
- ¼ teaspoon pepper
- 1 cup flour

Wash pieces of chicken and shake off excess water, but don't dry. Melt butter in large skillet, but don't let butter turn brown or burn. Combine dry ingredients and dredge chicken in the seasoned flour. Place chicken in skillet, cover, and over medium heat cook for 8 minutes then turn chicken. Reduce heat to very low and cook for about 30 minutes, turning 2 more times. Should be golden brown and crisp.

Serves 4.

CHICKEN LEGS PINWHEEL

    24 chicken legs
    1½ cups red wine
     2 cups bread crumbs
     1 tablespoon chopped fresh parsley
     1 teaspoon basil
     2 teaspoons oregano
    ½ teaspoon garlic powder
     1 teaspoon onion powder
     1 teaspoon salt
    ¼ teaspoon freshly ground pepper
     1 teaspoon Beau Monde seasoning

In large deep bowl combine bread crumbs, parsley, basil, oregano, garlic powder, onion powder, salt, pepper, and Beau Monde seasoning. Dip each chicken leg in wine then roll in bread-crumb mixture. Place legs on large shallow greased baking pan or cookie sheet covered with greased foil. Bake in preheated 350°F. oven for 40 to 50 minutes. Turn once during cooking. Place on round serving dish in a circle. Garnish with large bunch of parsley in the center.

Serves 12.

CHICKENSCHNITZEL

    4 chicken breasts, skinned and boned, halved
        and slightly flattened
    2 eggs plus 2 tablespoons water
      flour for dredging
      bread crumbs
      salt and pepper
    ½ cup vegetable oil and as needed
    1 lemon cut into wedges

Beat eggs with water in large shallow dish. Dredge
each chicken breast in flour and coat with egg mixture.
Dredge in bread crumbs and fry in heated oil two or
three pieces at a time. When golden on one side, turn
and brown on the other side. Transfer to heated
serving platter and keep warm. Add more oil as needed
until all chicken has been cooked. Garnish with lemon
wedges and parsley.

Serves 4.

CHILI-FLAVORED
FRIED CHICKEN

    1 3½-pound chicken, cut into 8 serving pieces
    2 tablespoons chili powder
    3 tablespoons oil
    1 medium onion—pureed in blender or forced
        through fine blade of food mill
    2 cloves garlic, crushed
    1 teaspoon lemon juice
      flour
      salt and pepper
    1½ cups oil

Blend chili powder, 3 tablespoons oil, pureed onion, crushed garlic, and lemon juice in large bowl. Add chicken and coat well with mixture. Cover and refrigerate overnight. Remove chicken from chili marinade and season with salt and pepper. Dredge in flour and fry in heated oil until golden on all sides, about 25 minutes total cooking time.

Serves 4.

CHINESE FRIED CHICKEN

    8 serving pieces of chicken
    ½ cup soy sauce
    ½ cup sherry
    1 teaspoon sugar
    2 medium onions, chopped
      flour
      oil for deep-fat frying

Combine soy sauce, sherry, sugar, and onion, then marinate chicken overnight in the refrigerator, covered. Turn a few times during this time. Drain and roll each piece of chicken in flour. Heat oil and deep-fat fry chicken for about 12 to 15 minutes until golden on all sides.

Accompany with fluffy white rice and a mixed zucchini, snowpea, and mushroom vegetable dish.

Serves 4.

CORNFLAKE-COATED
OVEN-FRIED CHICKEN

    1 3-pound chicken, cut into 8 serving pieces
    1 cup cornflake crumbs
    1 teaspoon salt
    ¼ teaspoon pepper
    ½ cup evaporated milk
    4 tablespoons melted butter

Combine cornflake crumbs, salt and pepper. Dip chicken in evaporated milk and roll in seasoned cornflake crumbs. Let set for a few minutes. Pour butter into shallow baking dish and arrange chicken in dish, skin side down. Bake in preheated 375°F. for 30 minutes. Turn and bake 20 minutes longer until crisp and tender.

Serves 4.

COUNTRY FRIED CHICKEN

    8 serving pieces of chicken
    1½ cups vegetable oil
       milk
       salt and pepper
       flour

Heat oil in large skillet. Dip chicken in milk and season with salt and pepper. Dredge in flour and add to heated oil. Fry over medium heat for 10 minutes on one side and turn. Cook 10 minutes and turn again. Lower heat and fry 10 minutes and turn once more.

After 5 minutes chicken should be very very crisp and brown all over.

Serves 4.

Accompany with black-eyed peas, mashed potatoes, and corn bread.

FRIED CHICKEN
WITH BANANAS

    8 serving pieces of chicken
      flour for dredging
    2 eggs
    1 tablespoon water
    1 tablespoon oil
      salt and pepper
      bread crumbs
      oil for deep-fat frying
    4 firm but ripe bananas

Dredge chicken in flour and dip in eggs beaten with water, oil, salt and pepper to taste. Roll in bread crumbs and deep-fat fry for about 20 minutes until golden all over. Transfer to heated serving platter and keep hot. Gently roll bananas in bread crumbs and fry like the chicken pieces, but only for a few moments until golden. Drain. Place on platter with chicken and garnish with parsley. Serve immediately.

Serves 4.

KENTUCKY FRIED CHICKEN

    1 3-pound chicken, cut into 8 serving pieces
    1 egg
    ½ cup milk
    1 cup flour
    1 teaspoon baking powder
    1 teaspoon salt
      pepper to taste
      oil for deep-fat frying

Mix together egg and milk. In a separate bowl combine flour, baking powder, salt and pepper. Pour egg mixture into dry ingredients. Beat for a few minutes until smooth. Dip chicken in batter and fry in hot deep fat until golden on all sides, about 15 minutes. Drain on absorbent paper.

Serves 4.

MARYLAND CHICKEN

    8 serving pieces chicken
      salt and pepper
      flour
    5 tablespoons oil
    2 tablespoons butter
    1 cup evaporated milk
      fresh chopped parsley

Season chicken with salt and pepper and dredge in flour. Heat oil and fry chicken until crisp and brown on all sides, about 30 to 35 minutes. Transfer chicken to heated serving dish. Pour off fat from skillet. Add 2

tablespoons butter and evaporated milk, bring to a
boil, and scrape up particles stuck on bottom of
skillet. Season well with salt and pepper. When sauce
thickens, pour over chicken. Garnish with parsley.

Serves 4.

OVEN-FRIED CHICKEN

1 3-pound chicken, cut into 8 serving pieces
  seasoned bread crumbs
4 tablespoons butter

In shallow baking dish place butter and melt in
400°F. oven. Coat chicken in seasoned bread crumbs.
Arrange chicken in melted butter skin side down. Bake
for ½ hour; turn and bake about 15 minutes more or
until crisp and tender.

Serves 4.

SESAME CHICKEN

1 3-pound chicken, cut into 8 serving pieces
3 eggs
2 tablespoons water
½ cup sesame seeds
¾ cup flour
  salt and pepper
6 tablespoons peanut or vegetable oil

Mix eggs and water. Coat pieces of chicken in
mixture. In flat dish blend sesame seeds and flour and

season with salt and pepper. Dredge chicken in flour and fry in heated oil until golden on all sides, about 30 minutes all together.

Serves 4.

SOUTHERN-FRIED CHICKEN WITH MILK GRAVY

1 3½-pound chicken, cut into serving pieces
  salt and pepper
  flour for dredging
2 cups lard
2 tablespoons butter
2 tablespoons flour for gravy
2 cups milk

Dip chicken in water, season with salt and pepper and roll in flour, shaking excess flour off. Let set for 5 minutes. Meanwhile, melt lard in large heavy skillet. When hot, but not smoking, add pieces of chicken and cook over medium heat until evenly browned on all sides, about 30 minutes. Drain on paper towels for a minute and transfer cooked chicken to serving dish and keep warm in preheated low oven. Pour off all fat except for about 1 tablespoon from skillet and add butter, scraping pan to pick up any crumbs. Sprinkle flour over pan, still stirring. Slowly pour in milk, always stirring. Should thicken and be smooth except for crumbs. Season highly with salt and pepper. Serve gravy in sauceboat and spoon generously over chicken. The gravy is also delicious on mashed potatoes or fresh biscuits.

Serves 4.

VIENNESE FRIED CHICKEN

1 3-pound chicken, quartered (backbone
   removed)
   salt and pepper
   flour
2 eggs, beaten
   bread crumbs
   oil for deep-fat frying
4 chicken livers
4 sprigs parsley
4 lemon wedges

Season chicken with salt and pepper. Dredge in
flour and coat with beaten eggs. Dip in bread crumbs.
Heat enough oil to have at least 1 inch in skillet. Fry
chicken until golden on both sides. Should take no
longer than 6 to 7 minutes on each side. Remove
chicken to absorbent paper and drain. Coat livers and
parsley in same manner as chicken with flour, egg,
bread crumbs and fry for a few minutes until crisp.
Serve each quarter of chicken with liver, parsley, and
lemon wedge.

Serves 4.

CHICKEN THE TRADITIONAL: ROASTED

A simple roast chicken properly cooked is superb. The secret is not to overcook the bird. Test for doneness by piercing the flesh part of the lower thigh. If the juices that are expelled have tinges of pink the bird still isn't cooked; but when juices run clear the bird is done. I'm particularly fond of French roast chicken in which the bird is stuffed and basted with butter and herbs. The flesh is juicy and succulent. A 4-to-4½-pound roasting chicken will serve 3 to 4. If more people are to be served either roast two birds or a 6-to-8-pound capon.

BASIC ROAST CHICKEN

1 4-pound roasting chicken
  salt and pepper
  butter for basting

Wash chicken and pat dry. Season cavity with salt and pepper. Truss bird and rub butter on breast and legs. Place in preheated 425°F. oven and roast for 15 minutes. Reduce heat to 350°F. and baste with butter. Roast for approximately 1 hour more, basting frequently (approximately 20 minutes per pound of chicken). Test for doneness by pricking the skin of the thickest flesh of the thigh; if the juice which spurts out is clear, it is done—if pink, not done. Or if leg and thigh move easily bird should be done.

Serves 4.

CHICKEN À LA BONNE FEMME

 1 3½-to-4-pound roasting chicken
    salt and pepper
 8 tablespoons butter, or as needed
 6 strips bacon, diced, blanched
18 small white onions
 2 cups potatoes, cut into small balls
 1 tablespoon Bovril

Place 3 tablespoons of butter in seasoned cavity of chicken and truss. Rub chicken with butter and place in heavy casserole, cover and cook in preheated 375°F. oven for ½ hour. Add bacon, onions, potatoes and 3 tablespoons butter, and roast uncovered for 25 to 30 minutes, basting frequently with butter, until chicken is tender and vegetables are cooked. Transfer chicken to serving platter and remove trussing string. Surround chicken with potatoes and onions. Add Bovril to juices in casserole and simmer for 2 or 3 minutes. Swirl in 2 tablespoons butter and pour strained sauce over chicken.

Serves 4.

CHICKEN À LA CONGO

1 3½-pound roasting chicken
1 stick butter or ¼ pound
1½ cups roasted peanuts, unsalted if possible,
    coarsely chopped
   salt
4 green peppers, stems removed and seeded
3 tablespoons oil
1 cup peanut butter

Heat oven to 350°F. Pack butter inside chicken along with ½ cup peanuts. Rub chicken with butter on skin side. Put in oven and baste occasionally. Meanwhile, cut green peppers into inch pieces and fry in very hot oil for 5 minutes, turning frequently. Let them almost burn. Take off heat and cool. When chicken has cooked ½ hour, surround chicken with cooked peppers. After 15 more minutes remove chicken and with a spatula spread peanut butter thinly over chicken. Sprinkle 1 cup of chopped nuts over chicken. They will stick to the peanut butter and form a prickly coat. Return to oven for another 10 to 15 minutes. Serve on platter surrounded by green peppers.

Serves 4.

Plain buttered rice goes well with this dish.

CHINESE ROAST CHICKEN

2 chicken breasts, halved
4 chicken legs
4 chicken thighs
3 tablespoons dark corn syrup
½ cup chili sauce
¼ cup ketchup
1 tablespoon Worcestershire sauce
½ cup soy sauce
1 medium onion, finely chopped
3 or 4 garlic cloves, crushed
½ teaspoon salt
2 tablespoons red food coloring

Combine ingredients in large bowl and marinate chicken for several hours. Remove from marinade and place on rack over a roasting pan filled with an inch of water. Place in preheated 325°F. oven for 20 minutes. Turn heat to 350°F. for 20 minutes and finally turn oven to 400°F. for 10 minutes until chicken is tender and beautifully reddish brown.

Serves 6.

FRENCH ROAST CHICKEN

1 3½-pound chicken
   salt and pepper
4 tablespoons butter
½ teaspoon tarragon
½ cup white wine
1 tablespoon flour
¾ cup chicken stock

Season body cavity of chicken with salt and pepper and put butter and tarragon inside bird. Sew opening closed, truss, and set in small roasting pan with wine. Place in preheated 325°F. oven and roast for 1 hour and 20 minutes or until tender, basting often with extra butter. Remove trussing string and let butter from chicken pour out into roasting pan. Make gravy by whisking flour into butter in pan and adding stock.

Serves 4.

GREEK LEMON ROAST CHICKEN

1 3-pound chicken
   salt and pepper
1 garlic clove, quartered
1 teaspoon dried oregano
3 tablespoons butter
1 tablespoon oil
   juice of 1 lemon—save lemon halves
½ cup chicken stock

Season cavity of chicken with salt and pepper. Place garlic and ½ teaspoon of dried oregano in chicken.

Sew up opening and truss. Melt butter with oil and brown chicken on all sides in low-sided casserole or roasting pan. Rub chicken with lemon halves and baste with butter and oil in which chicken was browned. Place in preheated 350°F. oven for 1 hour or until tender, basting frequently. Transfer to heated serving dish. Add lemon juice to roasting pan, bring to a boil on top of stove and add remaining ½ teaspoon oregano and chicken broth. Boil for 2 minutes, pour over chicken and serve.

Serves 4.

HONEY ROASTED CHICKEN

    1 3-to-3½-pound chicken, quartered
    6 tablespoons butter
    ½ cup honey
    2 tablespoons lime or lemon juice
      salt and pepper
    ½ cup toasted almond slivers (To toast, sauté
        almonds in 1 tablespoon butter for a few
        minutes until golden. Drain on absorbent
        paper.)

Melt butter and mix in honey and lime or lemon juice. Pat chicken dry with paper towels and season lightly with salt and pepper. Place in shallow dish and pour honey mixture over chicken. Marinate for several hours in refrigerator. Line roasting pan with aluminum foil and put chicken in pan skin side up. Reserve honey mixture for basting. Roast chicken in preheated 425°F. oven for 15 minutes. Turn, baste chicken with honey mixture, and cook 10 minutes more. Turn chicken again, baste, and lower heat to 375°. Cook for 15 minutes more. Sprinkle chicken pieces with toasted almonds and serve.

Serves 4.

POULET CLASSIQUE

    1 4-pound roasting chicken
    4 ounces butter or 1 stick
    4 shallots, minced
    2 garlic cloves, crushed
    ¾ cup fresh chopped parsley
    ½ teaspoon tarragon
    1 cup bread crumbs
    2 or 3 tablespoons Cognac
      salt and pepper to taste
 1½ cups chicken stock
    1 tablespoon flour
    3 tablespoons butter

Sauté shallots and garlic in 2 tablespoons butter for 5 minutes. Melt 6 more tablespoons butter with shallots and garlic and pour into large bowl. Combine with parsley, tarragon, bread crumbs, and Cognac for stuffing. Season to taste with salt and pepper. Break the membrane at the chicken's vent opening of the breast and insert finger between skin and meat. Work fingers along each side of breast, over legs and thighs being careful not to break skin over center of breast-bone. Spoon stuffing under loosened skin a tablespoon at a time. Work stuffing over leg, thigh and breast of chicken on each side evenly. Don't overstuff. If any stuffing is left over put it inside chicken.

Sew up vent opening and truss chicken. Place in roasting pan and add 1 cup chicken stock. Roast in preheated 350°F. oven for 1 hour and 20 minutes or until chicken is tender. Transfer chicken to heated platter and remove trussing strings. Place roasting pan over heat on top of stove and bring liquid to a boil, scraping up any particles on the side or bottom of pan. Sprinkle in flour stirring constantly and add remaining ½ cup chicken stock and bring to a boil again. Swirl in 3 tablespoons butter and cook for a minute or two. Serve in sauceboat.

Serves 4.

POULET VAN GOGH

- 1 3½-pound roasting chicken
- 8 slices bacon
- 2 tablespoons butter
- 1 medium onion, chopped
- 2 cups diced boiled potatoes
- 1 teaspoon wine vinegar
- 1 teaspoon paprika
  salt and pepper to taste

Cook 4 slices of bacon until crisp. Drain bacon, chop, and set aside. Pour all but 1 tablespoon of bacon drippings out of pan. Melt butter with bacon drippings in pan and sauté chopped onion for about 5 minutes. Transfer to bowl. Add crumbled bacon, diced potatoes, wine vinegar, paprika, and salt and pepper to taste. Carefully combine for stuffing and let cool slightly. Meanwhile, wash bird and pat dry. Stuff body cavity with potato stuffing and truss. Place remaining 4 slices of bacon over breast of chicken and secure with string or toothpicks. Roast in preheated 350°F. oven for 1 hour or until chicken is tender. Baste with pan juices occasionally. Remove string or toothpicks holding bacon on chicken and trussing string.

Serves 4.

ROAST CHICKEN
FILLED WITH MASHED POTATOES

   1 4½-to-5-pound roasting chicken
2½ cups mashed potatoes
   2 tablespoons minced onions
   2 tablespoons melted butter
   1 teaspoon salt
      pinch of nutmeg
   ¼ teaspoon white pepper
   1 cup chicken broth

Combine mashed potatoes, minced onions, butter, salt, pepper, and nutmeg. Stuff chicken; sew opening closed and truss. Rub butter or oil over chicken. Place in preheated 400°F. oven for 30 minutes. Add chicken broth, reduce heat to 350°F., and cook 45 minutes longer or until done.

Serves 4 to 6.

ROAST CHICKEN WITH
HONEY AND PISTACHIO NUTS

1 3½-pound roasting chicken
2 tablespoons butter
2 tablespoons honey
¼ cup pistachio nuts, chopped fine
¼ cup crystallized cherries, chopped
⅛ cup chopped preserved ginger

Melt butter and add honey. Prick the breast and legs of bird with sharp pointed fork. Rub chicken inside and out with butter and honey mixture. Place in preheated 350°F. oven and roast about 1 hour or until tender. Cut chicken into quarters and sprinkle with mixture of pistachio nuts, cherries, and ginger.

Serves 4.

ROAST CHICKEN WITH
WATERCRESS STUFFING

1 3½-pound chicken
5 tablespoons butter
1 tablespoon oil
1 medium onion, finely chopped
1 stalk celery, finely chopped
1 tablespoon lemon juice
1 bunch fresh watercress, finely chopped
½ cup bread crumbs
  salt and pepper to taste

Melt 2 tablespoons butter with oil and cook onion and celery for 3 or 4 minutes. Add remaining butter and lemon juice. Stir in watercress and bread crumbs and season with salt and pepper. Cool slightly and use to stuff chicken. Sew up vent and truss bird. Roast in preheated 350°F. oven for 1 hour or until tender.

Serves 4.

SPIT-ROASTED CHICKEN

A 2-pound broiler will easily serve 2 people. Rub chickens with butter and a little tarragon. Truss birds firmly, fitting two or three birds on a spit. Balance them on the spit so they will cook evenly. Roast 45 minutes to 1 hour depending on size of birds. Baste often with butter mixed with a little paprika, Lawry's Seasoned Salt, or curry. Serve with baked potatoes, corn on the cob, and a tossed green salad.

CHICKEN THE TRADITIONAL: SAUTÉED

Sautéeing is probably the easiest method of cooking chicken. The best birds for sautés are frying chickens weighing 2½ to 3½ pounds. If available, fresh chickens should be the first choice. There are many ways to prepare sautéed chicken but the basic way is to first sauté the chicken portions in butter and/or oil over medium heat until chicken browns. Herbs, spices, and sometimes vegetables are added. The sauce is made later by adding shallots and wine. A sauté is accomplished in one pan on top of the stove—that alone makes it appealing to most cooks—and the preparation time is short. A delicious dish can be prepared in 25 to 45 minutes—one that requires only a little attention while you set the table, cook the vegetables, and toss the salad.

CHICKEN AND FENNEL SEEDS

- 1 3-pound chicken, cut into 8 serving pieces
  salt and pepper
- 3 tablespoons butter
- 2 tablespoons vegetable oil
- 3 shallots, minced
- 1 tablespoon fennel seeds—crush in mortar
  with pestle
- 1½ tablespoons flour
- ½ cup chicken broth
- ½ cup dry vermouth
- 2 teaspoons tomato paste

Season chicken with salt and pepper. Melt butter with oil in large skillet and brown chicken on all sides a few pieces at a time. Add more butter and oil if necessary. Return chicken to pan, add shallots, crushed fennel seeds, and sprinkle flour over chicken. Turn each piece. Pour broth and vermouth over chicken and stir in tomato paste. Bring to a boil. Cover and simmer for 35 minutes until chicken is tender.

Serves 4.

CHICKEN BELGIUM

- 1 3-pound chicken, cut into 8 serving pieces
- 4 tablespoons butter
- 4 leeks, sliced thin
- ¼ pound mushrooms, sliced
  giblets from chicken
- 1 cup chicken broth
- ½ cup heavy cream
- ¼ cup brandy
- 1 tablespoon tarragon
  salt and pepper to taste

Melt butter in skillet and, when foaming subsides, add chicken seasoned with salt and pepper and brown on all sides. Add leeks to pan and sauté for 5 minutes. Add mushrooms, uncooked giblets, and 1 cup chicken broth. Cover and simmer for 30 minutes. Remove giblets to plate and cool. Place chicken on side dish, then strain sauce. Return sauce to cleaned pan with finely chopped giblets, cream, brandy, and tarragon. Heat thoroughly. Add chicken and simmer for a few minutes. Adjust seasoning.

Serves 4.

CHICKEN CHASSEUR

1 2½-to-3-pound chicken cut into 8 serving
    pieces
2 tablespoons butter
2 tablespoons oil
2 tablespoons shallots, minced
½ pound mushrooms, quartered
2 tablespoons flour
1 cup Chablis or other dry white wine
½ teaspoon fresh chopped parsley
    pinch of thyme
1 bay leaf
2 large tomatoes, peeled, seeded, and chopped
½ teaspoon dried tarragon
    salt and pepper to taste

Melt butter with oil in casserole and brown chicken quickly on all sides. Remove chicken to side dish. Add shallots and mushrooms to casserole and cook, covered, for 5 minutes. Sprinkle flour over mushroom mixture and add remaining ingredients including browned chicken. Cover and simmer for 25 minutes or until tender.

Serves 4.

Serve in large serving dish with parslied new potatoes and whole green beans.

CHICKEN IN ORANGE SAUCE

    8 serving pieces chicken
    2 tablespoons butter
    1 tablespoon oil
    1 cup chicken stock
    ½ cup orange juice
    1 tablespoon grated orange rind
    1 teaspoon lemon juice
    1 tablespoon cornstarch
      salt and pepper to taste

Melt butter with oil. When hot, but not smoking, brown chicken on all sides. Add stock, orange juice, grated orange rind, and lemon juice. Bring to a boil, reduce heat and simmer for 35 minutes. Place chicken in warmed serving dish. Dissolve cornstarch in a little water and stir into sauce. Bring to a boil and cook for 2 to 3 minutes. Season and pour over chicken.

Serves 4.

CHICKEN IN SWEET VERMOUTH

1 2½-to-3-pound chicken, cut into 8 serving
    pieces
  salt and pepper
3 to 4 tablespoons butter
1 medium onion, sliced
½ cup sweet vermouth
1 tablespoon tomato paste
¼ teaspoon cinnamon
  pinch nutmeg

Season chicken with salt and pepper. Brown pieces
evenly in melted butter. Add remaining ingredients
and bring to a boil, cover and simmer for 25 minutes
turning once during cooking.

Serves 4.

CHICKEN NORMANDY

- 1 3-pound chicken, cut into 8 serving pieces
  salt and pepper
- 3 tablespoons butter
- 1 medium-large onion, sliced
- ¼ pound mushrooms, quartered
- 2 tart cooking apples, peeled, cored, and sliced
- 1 cup apple juice
- ¼ cup Calvados or brandy
- 2 tablespoons flour

Season chicken with salt and pepper. Melt butter and brown chicken on all sides. Add onion and sauté for 5 minutes, then add mushrooms and more butter if necessary. Simmer for 5 minutes. Add apples; pour in apple juice with Calvados or brandy. Bring to a boil, cover and simmer 35 minutes until tender. Adjust seasoning. Transfer chicken, apples, and mushrooms to serving dish, leaving as much liquid as possible in pan. Mix flour with enough water to make smooth paste and stir into hot sauce. Cook briskly for 2 to 3 minutes, whisking constantly. Adjust seasoning and pour over chicken and serve.

Serves 4.

CHICKEN SAUTÉED WITH HERBS

8 serving pieces chicken
   salt and pepper
½ stick or 2 ounces butter
1 tablespoon oil
4 shallots, minced
1 tablespoon lemon juice
¼ cup dry white wine
1 tablespoon chopped parsley
1 teaspoon chervil
1 teaspoon tarragon

Season chicken with salt and pepper. Brown chicken in butter and oil then add shallots. Cook for 3 minutes. Sprinkle lemon juice, wine, and herbs over chicken. Cover and cook for 15 minutes. Turn chicken and cook 15 minutes longer, partially covered.

Serves 4.

CHICKEN SAUTÉ WITH MORELS
(*Poulet Sauté aux Morilles*)

6 medium chicken breasts, skinned, boned, and split
   salt and white pepper
8 tablespoons butter
⅓ cup brandy
1¾ cups heavy cream
1 heaping tablespoon Bovril
½ pound fresh morels or one 8-ounce can morels (or mushrooms) (reserve ¼ cup liquid from can)

Sprinkle chicken breasts with salt and pepper. Melt 4 tablespoons butter in skillet and sauté a few pieces of chicken at a time until golden brown on each side. Add butter as needed. Transfer breasts to warmed serving dish as they are cooked. When all breasts are browned, add brandy to skillet, heat, and (standing well back) ignite. When flame goes out, add cream and Bovril, stirring with whisk. Add morels and ¼ cup morel liquid if canned morels are used. Return chicken to sauce and simmer for 5 minutes.

Serves 6.

CHICKEN STANLEY SAUTÉ

1 3-pound chicken, cut into 8 serving pieces
4 tablespoons butter
3 medium onions, sliced
¼ pound mushrooms, sliced
¾ cup heavy cream
1 teaspoon curry powder
1 teaspoon lemon juice
½ teaspoon salt
1 truffle, sliced thin (optional)

Melt butter in large skillet and brown chicken on all sides. Add onions and cook for 15 minutes, covered. Add mushrooms and re-cover. Meanwhile, combine heavy cream, curry powder, lemon juice, and salt. Pour over chicken and simmer for 15 to 20 minutes more. Garnish with truffle slices.

Serves 4.

CHICKEN TARRAGON

8 serving pieces chicken
2 tablespoons butter
1 tablespoon bacon drippings
   salt and pepper
1 small onion, chopped
2 shallots, minced
1 cup chicken broth
1 cup dry white wine
1 bay leaf
1 tablespoon tarragon
1 tablespoon flour
1 tablespoon butter
½ cup heavy cream
   fresh chopped parsley

Melt butter with bacon drippings in deep heavy skillet or ovenproof casserole. Season chicken with salt and pepper and brown on all sides. Add onion with shallots and sauté for about 5 minutes. Add chicken broth, wine, bay leaf, and tarragon. Bring to a boil, reduce heat, and simmer for 45 minutes. Blend flour and butter together, then add cream and a few table-spoons of hot tarragon broth. Pour cream mixture into chicken and bring to a boil and simmer for 5 minutes. Sauce should thicken and coat chicken nicely. Transfer to heated serving dish and sprinkle with parsley.

Serves 4.

CHICKEN WITH RIESLING

    1 2½-to-3-pound chicken cut into 8 serving
        pieces
      salt and pepper to taste
    3 tablespoons butter
    2 tablespoons oil
    4 shallots, chopped
    ½ pound fresh mushrooms, quartered
    3 tomatoes, peeled, seeded, and chopped
    1 cup Riesling
    2 tablespoons brandy
    2 tablespoons heavy cream
    1 teaspoon fresh chopped parsley

Season chicken with salt and pepper, then brown on all sides in butter and oil. Add shallots, mushrooms, and tomatoes. Simmer for a few minutes, then pour in Riesling and brandy, cover, and simmer for 25 minutes. Turn once during cooking. Transfer chicken to heated serving dish and keep warm. Skim off as much fat as possible from liquid in pan. Add heavy cream and parsley. Check seasoning. Pour sauce over chicken.

Serves 4.

CHICKEN WITH SHALLOTS

8 serving pieces of chicken
4 tablespoons butter
2 tablespoons oil
3 dozen whole shallots, peeled
  salt and pepper
1 teaspoon lemon juice
½ cup chicken broth

Melt butter in large skillet and add oil. When heated, brown chicken a few pieces at a time on all sides, then transfer to side dish. When all chicken has been browned, add shallots to pan and sauté for 5 minutes, shaking pan often. Return chicken to skillet and season with salt and pepper. Cover and simmer for 30 minutes. Transfer chicken and shallots to warmed serving dish; add lemon juice and broth to skillet and scrape up any particles left in pan and bring to a boil, adjust seasoning, and pour over chicken.

Serves 4.

CHICKEN WITH SPINACH CREAM SAUCE AND BACON

8 serving pieces chicken
salt and pepper
flour
2 tablespoons butter, or as needed
2 tablespoons oil, or as needed
8 bacon slices, cut into 2-inch pieces
1 medium onion, chopped
2 tablespoons sherry
1 cup chicken broth
1 cup fresh chopped spinach—if frozen is used, thaw and dry in paper towels as much as possible
¾ cup heavy cream

Season chicken with salt and pepper and dredge in flour. Shake off any excess flour. In skillet melt butter with oil. When hot but not smoking, brown chicken well on all sides, a few pieces at a time, adding butter and oil as needed. Transfer to side dish as chicken pieces are browned. When all chicken is browned, discard remaining fat. Put bacon in pan and cook until crisp. Drain on paper towels. Pour off all fat but 1 tablespoon. Add onion and cook for 4 or 5 minutes, stirring. Pour in sherry and bring to a boil. Add broth, chicken, and spinach. Reduce heat, cover, and simmer for 20 minutes or until chicken is tender.

Remove chicken to warmed serving dish. Add cream to sauce and bring to a boil. Reduce heat and simmer for a few moments. Pour sauce over chicken and sprinkle with crisp bacon.

Serves 4.

CHICKEN WITH THYME

1 3-pound chicken cut into 8 serving pieces
    salt and pepper
2 tablespoons butter
1 tablespoon vegetable oil
1 garlic clove, minced
1 medium onion, chopped
1 teaspoon thyme
1 cup chicken broth
1 chicken bouillon cube
¾ cup dry white wine
1 tablespoon flour
    fresh chopped parsley

Dry chicken pieces thoroughly and season with salt and pepper. Melt butter with oil in skillet. Brown chicken on all sides and transfer to side dish. Add garlic and onion to skillet and sauté for 5 minutes. Now add thyme, chicken broth, bouillon cube, and wine. Bring to a boil, add chicken, reduce heat to a simmer and cook for ½ hour. Remove chicken to warm serving dish and cover to keep warm. Strain sauce in skillet and put into saucepan. Blend flour with enough water to make smooth paste and whisk into sauce. Bring to a boil and pour over chicken. Garnish with fresh chopped parsley.

Serves 4.

COUNTRY CAPTAIN

This dish from India probably received it's name because a sea captain brought the recipe back to the States.

1 2½-to-3-pound chicken, cut into 8
    serving pieces
  salt and pepper
  flour for dredging
3 tablespoons butter
1 tablespoon bacon drippings
1 medium onion, chopped
½ medium green pepper, diced
1 clove garlic, crushed
½ teaspoon thyme
2 tablespoons curry powder
2 cups canned tomatoes and juice, chopped
2 tablespoons dried currants
½ cup toasted almond slivers

Season chicken with salt and pepper and dredge in flour. Melt butter with bacon drippings in large frypan and brown chicken pieces on all sides. Transfer chicken to dish. Add onion, green pepper, garlic, thyme, and curry powder to skillet and sauté until onion is transparent. Add tomatoes and return chicken to pan. Cover and simmer for ½ hour. Add currants during last few minutes of cooking. Serve on rice and garnish with toasted almond slivers.

Serves 4.

HERBED CITRUS CHICKEN

   8 serving pieces chicken
   ½ cup flour
   1 teaspoon salt
   ¼ teaspoon pepper
   ½ teaspoon paprika
   2 tablespoons butter
   2 tablespoons oil
   1 medium onion, finely chopped
   ¼ cup fresh chopped parsley
   ½ teaspoon dried thyme
   ½ teaspoon dried marjoram
   2 tablespoons lemon juice
   1 teaspoon grated lemon rind

Combine flour, salt, pepper, and paprika. Dredge chicken pieces in seasoned flour. Melt butter with oil and brown chicken on all sides. Add onion, parsley, thyme, marjoram, lemon juice, and grated lemon rind. Cover and cook slowly for 25 minutes, turning chicken once during cooking.

Serves 4.

LYONNAISE CHICKEN WITH PARSLEY BUTTER

4 chicken legs
4 chicken thighs
   salt and pepper
5 tablespoons butter
1 large onion, cut into thin 2-inch slivers
½ cup chicken stock

PARSLEY BUTTER

1 stick butter or ¼ pound
4 tablespoons finely chopped fresh parsley

Melt 3 tablespoons butter in skillet. Dry chicken thoroughly and season lightly with salt and pepper. Brown chicken on each side. Add 2 remaining tablespoons butter, onion, and broth, cover and simmer until chicken is tender, about 25 minutes. Meanwhile, prepare parsley butter. Clarify butter by melting it and pour clear butter from pan leaving white sediment in bottom of pan. Put clarified butter in clean saucepan, add parsley, and simmer for 4 to 5 minutes. Set aside. Adjust seasoning of chicken and onions. Transfer chicken and onions to heated serving dish. Pour heated parsley butter over chicken and serve immediately.

Serves 4.

Serve with oven roasted potatoes.

MARINATED CHICKEN SAUTÉ

1 3-pound chicken, cut into serving pieces
2 Spanish onions, chopped
1 garlic clove, crushed
1 cup red wine
1 bay leaf
  salt and pepper
  flour
2 tablespoons butter
2 tablespoons oil

Place chicken in deep bowl, add onions, garlic, and wine. Cover and marinate in refrigerator overnight. Remove chicken from marinade and sprinkle with salt and pepper, then dredge in flour. Melt butter with oil and brown chicken on all sides for about 30 minutes until tender.

Serves 4.

MOROCCAN CHICKEN

1 3-pound chicken, cut into 8 serving pieces
3 tablespoons olive oil
1 medium-large onion, sliced
½ teaspoon turmeric
1 teaspoon ground ginger
2 teaspoons paprika or to taste
1 tablespoon lemon juice
1 cup chicken broth
    salt and pepper to taste
½ cup green olives, cut into slivers
8 thin slices fresh lemon—seeds removed

Heat oil in large skillet and brown chicken evenly a few pieces at a time. Remove to side dish as browned. Add onion and sauté for 5 or 6 minutes until transparent. Sprinkle turmeric, ginger, paprika, and lemon juice on onions. Stir a little, then add chicken and pour broth into pan. Bring to a boil, reduce heat, cover, and simmer for ½ hour. Adjust seasoning and add olives and lemon slices. Cover and simmer for 5 minutes.

Serves 4.

POULET A L'AIL
(Chicken with Garlic)

1 3-pound chicken, cut into 8 serving pieces
salt and pepper
5 tablespoons butter
1 tablespoon oil
10 cloves garlic, peeled and crushed
½ cup dry white wine
1 cup chicken stock, heated
3 tablespoons heavy cream
1 tablespoon flour

Season chicken with salt and pepper. In a large skillet, brown chicken on all sides in 3 tablespoons butter and oil. Cover, reduce heat, and simmer for 10 minutes. Transfer chicken to heated plate and cover to keep hot. Add 2 tablespoons butter with garlic, cook for 5 to 8 minutes, stirring occasionally, until garlic is quite limp. Pour in white wine and bring to a boil. Replace chicken in skillet and add chicken stock. Cover and simmer for about 15 minutes. Combine heavy cream and flour and add a tablespoon or two of hot liquid from skillet to cream mixture. Blend, then pour into skillet, stirring constantly. Place chicken on heated serving dish. Strain sauce and pour over chicken. Garnish with fresh chopped parsley.

Serves 4.

RED CHICKEN

1 3-pound chicken, cut into 8 serving pieces
  salt and pepper
3 tablespoons olive oil
2 medium onions, chopped
2 garlic cloves, minced
½ teaspoon basil
¼ teaspoon thyme
½ teaspoon marjoram
2 tablespoons butter
1 large red pepper, cut into thin strips
2 medium tomatoes, peeled, seeded and
  cut into thin strips
2 tablespoons concentrated orange juice
½ teaspoon red food coloring

Skin chicken and season with salt and pepper. Brown in heated olive oil on all sides. Add onions, garlic, basil, thyme, and marjoram. Cover and simmer for 20 minutes. Meanwhile, melt butter in another skillet and cook red pepper strips for 5 minutes. Add tomatoes, orange juice concentrate, and red food coloring. Correct seasoning. When chicken has cooked for 20 minutes, pour pepper mixture over chicken and turn each piece, cover and simmer for 10 to 15 minutes until chicken is tender. Serve on fluffy white rice.

Serves 4.

SAUTÉED CHICKEN DEMI-DEUIL

1 2½-pound chicken
   salt and pepper
3 tablespoons butter
2 tablespoons flour
1 cup chicken stock
3 tablespoons heavy cream
1 egg, beaten
1 truffle, thinly sliced (optional)
½ cup chopped mushrooms

Cut chicken in half and remove backbone. Season with salt and pepper. Melt butter and brown chicken. Sprinkle with flour and turn each piece and sauté for 5 minutes. Add chicken stock and bring to a boil, reduce heat, and simmer, covered, until chicken is tender, about 25 minutes. Transfer chicken to heated platter. Mix cream with egg and add to sauce. Don't boil. Season. Add sliced truffle and mushrooms, cover and simmer for 5 minutes, but don't boil, and pour over chicken.

Serves 2.

SAUTÉED CHICKEN PANURGE

- 1 2½-to-3-pound chicken, cut into
      8 serving pieces
- salt and pepper
- 3 tablespoons butter
- ½ cup diced carrots
- ½ cup diced celery
- ½ cup chopped onions
- 1 tablespoon finely chopped parsley
- ½ cup dry white wine
- ½ cup chicken stock
- ¼ cup heavy cream
- ½ cup black olives, cut into thin slivers

Melt butter and brown chicken seasoned with salt and pepper on all sides. Transfer to side dish. Add carrots, celery, onions, and parsley. Sauté for 3 or 4 minutes. Return chicken to skillet on top of vegetables. Pour in wine and chicken stock. Bring to a boil, add cream, and return to a boil. Reduce heat, cover, and simmer for 25 minutes. Correct seasoning. Add olives, re-cover, and simmer for 5 minutes longer. Transfer to serving dish and garnish with toasted triangles of bread.

Serves 4.

SAUTÉED CHICKEN SABINESE

1 2½-to-3-pound chicken, cut into
    8 serving pieces
  pepper to taste
3 tablespoons olive oil
2 cloves garlic, crushed
1 medium onion, finely chopped
1 tablespoon wine vinegar
½ cup dry white wine
½ cup chicken stock
1 bay leaf
¼ teaspoon oregano
1 tablespoon capers
¼ cup sliced black olives
3 anchovy fillets—soaked in milk, rinsed,
    drained, and chopped

Season chicken with pepper. In large skillet heat olive oil and brown chicken on all sides. As chicken is browned, set aside. Add garlic and onion. Cook for 5 or 6 minutes until transparent. Add vinegar, wine, and stock, bring to a boil and cook for 2 or 3 minutes. Return chicken to pan, add bay leaf and oregano, cover, then simmer for 25 minutes. Sprinkle capers, black olives, and anchovies over chicken and stir into sauce. Cover and cook 5 minutes longer. Correct seasoning.

Serves 4.

SAUTÉED CHICKEN WITH BASIL

1 2½-to-3-pound chicken, cut into 8 serving pieces
  salt and pepper
3 tablespoons butter
1 cup dry white wine
1 tablespoon lemon juice
2 teaspoons dried basil

Season chicken well with salt and pepper. Melt butter in skillet and brown chicken on all sides. Transfer to side dish as chicken is browned. Pour in wine, bring to a boil, and reduce to half. Return chicken to skillet, add lemon juice and basil. Cover and simmer for 25 minutes. Adjust seasoning.

Serves 4.

SAUTÉED CHICKEN WITH YOGHURT AND CELERY SEEDS

1 3-pound chicken, cut into 8 serving pieces
2 tablespoons butter
2 tablespoons oil
  salt
1 tablespoon celery seeds
1 tablespoon flour
½ cup dry white wine
½ cup chicken broth
¾ cup plain yoghurt

Melt butter with oil and brown seasoned chicken on all sides. Sprinkle with celery seeds and flour. Turn each chicken piece. Add wine and chicken broth, cover and cook for 30 minutes. Transfer chicken to heated serving dish or platter. Whisk in yoghurt and heat thoroughly, but don't boil. Correct seasoning. Pour over chicken.

Serves 4.

SAUTÉED STUFFED CHICKEN BREASTS

4 chicken breasts, skinned, boned, and halved
  salt and pepper
8 slices Gruyère or Cheddar cheese
8 thin slices tongue
  flour
1 egg, beaten with 2 tablespoons water
  bread crumbs
6 tablespoons oil, or as needed

Make slit in side of each chicken breast half, forming a small pocket. Season with salt and pepper. Fill each pocket with a slice of cheese and a slice of tongue. Fold cheese and meat if necessary. Close opening with toothpick. Dredge in flour and coat with beaten egg with water and roll in bread crumbs. Fry in heated oil until golden on each side, about 7 minutes per side or less. Remove toothpicks. Arrange on heated serving dish and garnish with thin slices of lemon sprinkled with fresh chopped parsley.

Serves 4 to 6.

CHICKEN WITH A FOREIGN ACCENT

It is always interesting to experiment with a new dish and chicken recipes from foreign countries offer incredible variety. Some are easy to prepare; others take time and patience but prove wonderfully rewarding. They bring a difference and a distinction to your table. Most countries have a particular style of cooking and special local herbs and spices are invariably used— but all have been adapted to your kitchen in the recipes that follow.

ARROZ CON POLLO
(Chicken with Rice)

    1 3-pound chicken, cut into 8 serving pieces
      salt and pepper
    ⅓ cup olive oil
    1 large onion, coarsely chopped
    2 or 3 garlic cloves, minced
    1 teaspoon paprika
    3 cups chicken broth
    1 chicken bouillon cube
    1 large tomato, chopped
    ¼ teaspoon saffron
    1 bay leaf
 1½ cups rice
    1 cup green peas
    ½ teaspoon salt
    1 tablespoon freshly chopped parsley
    2 pimientos, cut into thin strips

Completely dry chicken with paper towels and season with salt and pepper. Heat oil in 4-or-5-quart ovenproof casserole and brown chicken on all sides. Transfer to side dish. Sauté onion and garlic for 5 minutes, stirring often. Sprinkle paprika over onions, add broth, bouillon cube, tomato, saffron, and bay leaf. Bring to a boil. Return chicken to casserole and simmer for 10 minutes. Add rice, peas, and salt. Stir gently, cover, and simmer for 25 to 30 minutes, or until chicken is tender and rice has absorbed liquid. Remove from heat. Sprinkle parsley over top and arrange strips of pimiento attractively. Cover and let stand 5 minutes before serving.

Serves 4.

ASOPAO
(Cuban Chicken Stew)

1 3½-pound chicken, cut into 8 serving pieces
3 tablespoons olive oil
1 large onion, chopped
3 garlic cloves, minced
1 green pepper, chopped
2 celery stalks, chopped
2 carrots, scraped and chopped
1 tablespoon fresh chopped parsley
2 tablespoons tomato paste
1 teaspoon oregano
1 cup cubed sweet potatoes
½ cup green peas
    chicken stock to cover
1 cup uncooked rice

Heat oil in large heavy casserole or Dutch oven. Sauté onion and garlic for 5 minutes. Add green pepper, celery, carrots, and parsley. Simmer for about 5 minutes. Add tomato paste and oregano. Gently blend and add chicken, sweet potatoes, and peas. Just cover ingredients in pot with chicken stock. Bring to a boil, reduce heat, and simmer covered for 30 minutes. Add rice, return to a boil, lower heat and simmer, covered, until rice is tender, about 30 minutes more. Serve with crusty bread.

Serves 4.

CAZUELA
(Chilean Chicken Stew)

    1 5-to-6-pound stewing fowl, cut into
         serving pieces
      flour
    4 tablespoons olive oil
    1 tablespoon fresh chopped parsley
    1 stalk celery, finely chopped
      pinch of thyme
    1 medium onion, chopped
    8 medium potatoes, peeled and left whole
    1 cup green peas
    1 cup green beans, cut
    1 small pumpkin, peeled, seeded, and cut in
         2-inch pieces
  ½ cup uncooked rice
    2 ears of corn—cut into 6 pieces each
      salt and pepper

Dredge chicken in flour and brown in heated olive oil. Place chicken in heavy casserole and cover with

cold water. Add parsley, celery, thyme, and onion.
Bring to a boil, reduce heat, and simmer for 1 hour.
Add potatoes and continue cooking for 30 minutes.
Next add pumpkin, peas, beans, rice, corn and cook
about 25 minutes or until rice is tender. Add a little
more water if necessary. Season with salt and pepper.
Remove from heat and let stand for 5 minutes. Serve
in soup plates and garnish with fresh chopped parsley.

Serves 6.

CHICKEN CACCIATORE

    1 3-pound chicken, cut into 8 serving pieces
      salt and pepper
 ¼ cup olive oil
    2 medium onions, sliced
    2 cloves garlic, minced
    1 green pepper—seeds removed—chopped
 ½ cup white wine
    1 tablespoon wine vinegar
    3 tomatoes, peeled, seeded, and chopped
 ½ cup chicken stock
 ½ teaspoon thyme
 ½ teaspoon oregano
    1 bay leaf
 ¼ pound mushrooms, sliced
      fresh chopped parsley

Heat oil in skillet and season chicken with salt and
pepper. Brown chicken on all sides and remove to side
dish. Add onions, garlic, and green pepper. Sauté for
8 minutes, transfer to side dish with chicken. Add wine
and wine vinegar and boil until reduced by half. Add
chicken stock and boil for a moment longer. Return

chicken and onion mixture to pan. Add tomatoes, oregano, and bay leaf. Cover and simmer for 30 minutes. Add mushrooms and cook 15 minutes longer. Season, remove bay leaf, and garnish with fresh chopped parsley.

Serves 4.

CHICKEN CHOP SUEY

2 cups raw chicken, cut into inch pieces
2 tablespoons peanut or vegetable oil
salt and pepper
1 cup drained bean sprouts
12 fresh mushrooms, sliced
½ cup sliced water chestnuts
3 stalks celery, chopped
¾ cup sliced onions

SAUCE

1½ tablespoons soy sauce
½ teaspoon sugar
1 tablespoon cornstarch
2 tablespoons sherry
½ cup water

Heat oil in skillet. When hot but not smoking, add chicken and salt and pepper. Turn as chicken browns, then add remaining ingredients. Cover and simmer for 15 minutes. Mix sauce and pour into chop suey. Stir until sauce thickens slightly. Serve on rice and sprinkle fried noodles on top.

Serves 4.

CHICKEN CUTLETS POJARSKY

It is argued whether these cutlets are named after an inn on the road between Moscow and Saint Petersburg where they were served, or after a seventeenth-century Russian general. Whatever their origin, they are both elegant and easy. Cutlets Pojarsky are rarely seen on restaurant menus, so they will provide a rare treat for guests.

    4 chicken breasts, skinned, boned, and
        ground very fine in meat grinder
    2 cups white bread cubes—crusts removed
    ¼ cup milk
    4 tablespoons vodka
    ½ cup heavy cream
    1 stick butter or ¼ pound
        pinch nutmeg
    1 teaspoon salt
    ¼ teaspoon white pepper
    1 cup flour
    2 eggs beaten with 3 tablespoons water
    1 cup dried bread crumbs or as needed
    ½ cup clarified butter*
    2 tablespoons oil

If you don't have a meat grinder have your butcher skin, bone, and grind the chicken breasts. Soak bread cubes in combined milk, vodka, and cream for 5 minutes. Squeeze out most of excess liquid. Bread cubes shouldn't be soggy. Combine chicken, bread,

---

* Clarify butter by melting it over heat and letting it stand for a few minutes. Skim off froth that rises and carefully pour clear butter out of pan leaving milky sediment in bottom of pan.

softened butter, nutmeg, salt and pepper, and mix
thoroughly. Place mixture on wax paper in dish and
cover. Refrigerate for ½ hour. Divide chicken mixture
into 12 sections, form each in the shape of a loin cutlet
about 1 inch thick and 3½ inches long. Dredge lightly
with flour. Dip each cutlet in egg and water mixture,
then coat with bread crumbs. Sauté in clarified butter
and oil until golden, about 4 to 5 minutes on each side.
Arrange on preheated serving dish and garnish each
cutlet with half a thin lemon slice, rind removed.
Serve with mushroom sauce (recipe follows).

MUSHROOM SAUCE

      3 tablespoons butter
      ¼ pound fresh mushrooms, finely chopped
      1 teaspoon lemon juice
      ¼ cup white wine
      ½ cup chicken broth
      ½ cup heavy cream
      2 teaspoons cornstarch
        salt and pepper

   Melt butter in saucepan and add mushrooms, lemon
juice, cover and simmer for 8 minutes. Add white wine,
chicken broth, and heavy cream. Bring to a boil, reduce
heat. Dissolve cornstarch in a little chicken broth and
stir into sauce. Season with salt and white pepper.
Simmer for a few minutes and serve in sauceboat with
cutlets.

Serves 6.

CHICKEN KIEV

Chicken Kiev, an elegant Russian dish created in the time of the czars, can be found on menus all over the world today. It is not difficult to prepare and there is something especially appealing about slicing into the chicken and watching the rich butter spurt out.

        4 chicken breasts, skinned, boned, and
            cut in half
     1½ sticks butter or 12 tablespoons
        ½ teaspoon lemon juice
        1 tablespoon chopped chives
        1 teaspoon dried tarragon
            salt and pepper
            flour
        2 eggs, beaten
        1 tablespoon water
            bread crumbs
            oil for deep frying

Mix softened butter with lemon juice, chives, and tarragon. Refrigerate for one hour. Place boned breasts between wax paper and pound flat. Careful not to break the flesh. Season with salt and pepper. Put a walnut-sized knob of butter in each breast and fold and roll chicken around butter. Chicken flesh should adhere to itself. Refrigerate for ½ hour.

Sprinkle flour over chicken and dip in beaten eggs with water and coat with bread crumbs. Cook in hot oil about 1½ inches deep until golden on all sides. Turn with tongs or spoon, but don't use fork because piercing the flesh would release the butter inside. Drain a few moments on absorbent paper. Place on

ovenproof serving dish and put in preheated 325°F.
oven for 10 minutes.

Serves 4 to 6.

CHICKEN LIVERS WITH MADEIRA

1 pound chicken livers, cleaned and cut in half
4 tablespoons butter
1 garlic clove, minced
¼ cup shallots, minced
1 tablespoon flour
1 cup chicken broth
¼ cup Madeira
 salt and pepper to taste
 fresh chopped parsley

Melt 2 tablespoons butter and sauté garlic and
shallots for 4 or 5 minutes, but don't brown. Sprinkle
flour over shallots and stir. Pour in chicken broth and
bring to a boil, always stirring. When sauce thickens,
lower heat and simmer for 5 minutes. Set aside and
cover. Melt remaining 2 tablespoons butter in skillet
and sauté livers for about 5 minutes over medium-high
heat until cooked. Transfer livers to heated dish and
pour Madeira into skillet in which livers cooked. Bring
to a boil, scraping bottom of pan, and reduce a little.
Slowly pour in shallot sauce, stirring constantly. Now
return livers and adjust seasoning. Garnish with fresh
chopped parsley.

Serves 4.

CHICKEN MALLORCAN STYLE

8 serving pieces chicken
3 tablespoons olive oil
3 cups sliced onions
2 cloves garlic, crushed
1 cup sherry
2 ripe tomatoes, peeled and chopped
   salt and pepper
   fresh chopped parsley

Heat olive oil in large skillet, Brown chickens on all sides and transfer to side dish. Add onions, garlic, and sherry to skillet and simmer until onions are transparent. Add tomatoes and season with salt and pepper. Place onion mixture in baking dish and arrange chicken pieces skin side down on onions. Bake in preheated 375°F. oven for 30 minutes. Turn chicken pieces and any onion that is browning. Cook 20 to 30 minutes more until chicken browns. Garnish with fresh chopped parsley.

Serves 4.

CHICKEN PAPRIKASH

1 3-pound chicken, cut into 8 serving pieces
3 tablespoons butter
2 medium onions, chopped
1½ tablespoons paprika
½ small red sweet pepper, seeded and minced
    (use green pepper if red pepper is not
    available)
1 teaspoon vinegar
½ teaspoon salt
    pepper
½ cup tomatoes, peeled and chopped
1 cup chicken stock
1 tablespoon flour
½ cup heavy cream
½ cup sour cream

Melt butter in large ovenproof casserole or Dutch oven. Sauté onion until transparent. Add paprika, red or green pepper, vinegar, and salt and pepper plus tomatoes and stock. Simmer for 5 minutes. Add chicken, cover, and cook slowly for 40 minutes until chicken is tender. Remove chicken to heated serving dish and cover. In small bowl blend flour with enough water to make a smooth paste and add to sauce along with cream, stirring gently. When sauce thickens slightly add sour cream but don't boil. Serve with egg noodles.

Serves 4.

CHICKEN PARMIGIANA

1 3-pound chicken, cut into 8 serving pieces
salt and pepper
3 tablespoons olive oil
½ teaspoon dried oregano
1 small green pepper, chopped
1 medium onion, sliced thin
8 large mushrooms, chopped
2 cloves garlic, crushed
6 tomatoes, peeled, seeded, and chopped
½ cup dry white wine
12 stuffed green olives, sliced
8 thin slices Mozzarella cheese
freshly grated Parmesan cheese

Season chicken with salt and pepper. Heat olive oil in large skillet and brown chicken on all sides. Add oregano, green pepper, onion, mushrooms, garlic, and tomatoes. Pour in white wine; bring to a boil, then reduce heat, cover, and simmer for 15 minutes. Turn chicken, add olives, and cook 10 minutes more. Adjust seasoning. Transfer chicken to a shallow baking dish and spoon ingredients from skillet over chicken. Place a slice of Mozzarella cheese over each piece of chicken. Broil under preheated broiler until cheese turns golden. Serve with fresh grated Parmesan cheese.

Serves 4.

CHICKEN PORTUGUESE STYLE

8 serving pieces chicken—dry with cloth so
    they will brown easily
4 tablespoons butter
2 medium onions, chopped
2 cloves garlic, minced
4 shallots, minced
4 tablespoons flour
1 cup white wine
2 cups chicken stock
    bouquet garni made of: 3 sprigs parsley,
        ½ teaspoon thyme, 1 bay leaf, and
        6 peppercorns
2 teaspoons tomato paste
    salt and pepper to taste
½ pound fresh mushrooms, sliced
½ cup black olives, pitted and cut into slivers
½ cup green olives (blanched), pitted, and
    cut into slivers
3 firm ripe tomatoes, peeled and cut into wedges
    (To peel tomatoes pour enough water to
    cover tomatoes in a saucepan and bring to
    a boil Submerge each tomato for 7 to 8
    seconds. Remove and skin can easily be
    peeled.)
    fresh chopped parsley

Heat butter in large skillet and brown chicken on
both sides. Add onions, garlic, and shallots and cook
for 5 minutes. Sprinkle flour over chicken and turn
each piece of chicken. Add wine and stock. Gently stir
with wooden spoon. Add bouquet garni and tomato
paste, season. Cover and simmer for 25 to 30 minutes.
Add mushrooms, black and green olives, and tomatoes.
Re-cover and simmer for 8 to 10 minutes longer. Re-

move bouquet garni and serve. Garnish with finely chopped fresh parsley.

Serves 4.

CHICKEN TANDOORI

1 3-pound chicken—quartered, backbone removed
1 cup plain yoghurt
3 or 4 cloves garlic, crushed
1 teaspoon ginger
1 teaspoon cinnamon
1 teaspoon cumin
1 teaspoon turmeric
2 teaspoons coriander
⅛ teaspoon cayenne pepper
¼ cup lime juice
    salt and pepper to taste
    butter
2 medium-large onions, sliced very thin
    Break onions apart into individual rings and deep-fat fry in an inch of hot oil until golden brown, then drain.
4 thin slices of lime

Combine yoghurt, garlic, ginger, cinnamon, cumin, turmeric, coriander, cayenne pepper, and lime juice. Prick chicken pieces all over with fork and marinate in yoghurt mixture overnight in the refrigerator, covered. Make sure all pieces of chicken are coated thoroughly and turn at least once while marinating. Place chicken in greased shallow baking dish, skin side up. Sprinkle a little melted butter over each piece of chicken and cook in 375°F. oven for 50 to 60 minutes, basting occasionally. Garnish with fried onions and a slice of lime for each quarter. Serve with rice.

Serves 4.

CIRCASSIAN CHICKEN
(*Turkish*)

1 3½-to-4-pound chicken
3 quarts water
1 large carrot, peeled and chopped
1 large onion, chopped
3 or 4 sprigs parsley
   salt and pepper
2 cups shelled walnuts
3 slices white bread
1 tablespoon paprika

Place chicken, carrots, onion, and parsley in water and bring to a boil. Skim. Season with salt and pepper. Cover and cook for 1½ hours until chicken is tender. Remove chicken and save stock. Remove skin and bones and cut chicken into small pieces. Put walnuts through grinder twice. Soak bread in a little of the reserved chicken stock. Squeeze dry and put in large bowl and add ground walnuts and paprika. Force mixture through meat grinder 3 times, add 1 cup chicken stock and work into consistency of paste. Blend ½ of paste with pieces of chicken and spread out on plate. Spread rest of paste over chicken mixture. Serve cold with crisp green salad.

Serves 4 to 6.

COQ AU VIN

Coq au Vin is one of the most famous chicken classics. I learned this particular recipe in Paris while watching a superb chef at work. It is one of my most treasured recipes.

  1 3½-pound chicken, cut into serving pieces
  4 tablespoons butter
  6 slices bacon, cut into 1-inch strips
16 small white onions, peeled and left whole
  2 medium onions, chopped
  4 shallots, chopped
  4 cloves garlic, minced
  3 tablespoons flour
  ½ bottle red Burgundy
  2 cups rich beef stock
    bouquet garni of: 1 bay leaf, 3 or 4 sprigs of parsley, pinch of thyme, and 6 peppercorns
  1 tablespoon tomato paste
    salt and pepper to taste
  8 tablespoons butter
  ½ pound mushrooms, quartered
  1 cup beef stock
  4 drops red food coloring
  2 tomatoes, peeled
  2 tablespoons brandy
    fresh chopped parsley

Melt 4 tablespoons butter in skillet and brown chicken on all sides over medium heat. Meanwhile, cook bacon in small pan of boiling water for 5 minutes. Drain. In another pan, with enough boiling water to cover, poach small whole onions for 8 to 10 minutes until just tender. When chicken has browned, add chopped onions, shallots, and garlic. Cook for 5 minutes. Sprinkle flour over chicken and turn each piece. Add wine, stock, bouquet garni, and tomato paste. Season, partially cover, and simmer for 30 minutes. In another skillet put 3 tablespoons butter and sauté poached onions over high heat until they have browned nicely. Remove to side dish. Clean skillet and add 2 tablespoons butter to skillet and brown bacon. Remove and drain. Now add 3 tablespoons of remaining butter to skillet and sauté mushrooms for 5 minutes over medium-high heat. Remove mushrooms to side dish with onions and bacon. When chicken has cooked 30 minutes, remove to platter. Strain sauce through fine sieve and reserve. Wash and dry large skillet. Return chicken and sauce to clean pan along with onions, bacon, and mushrooms. Add red food coloring. Cover and simmer for 10 minutes. Meanwhile, peel tomatoes and squeeze juice out and seeds. (To peel tomatoes, dip them in boiling water for 8 seconds and they will peel easily.) Add to chicken mixture 5 minutes before it is finished cooking and re-cover. Pour in brandy and stir. Remove chicken pieces to large serving dish and spoon sauce over chicken. Garnish with fresh chopped parsley.

Serves 4.

EAST INDIAN CHICKEN CURRY

1 3-pound chicken, cut into 8 serving pieces
1 tablespoon ground ginger
1 tablespoon curry powder
1 teaspoon allspice
2 teaspoons turmeric
  salt and pepper to taste
3 tablespoons butter
1 large onion, chopped
1 small green pepper, chopped
1 clove garlic, crushed
1 cup fresh tomatoes, chopped
2 cups beef stock
1 large tart cooking apple, peeled, cored,
  and chopped
1 cup green peas (optional)

Arrange chicken in large shallow dish and sprinkle with ginger, curry powder, allspice, turmeric, salt and pepper. Rub spices into chicken as evenly as possible. Let stand for 15 minutes. Meanwhile, melt butter in deep pan and sauté onions, green peppers, and garlic for 5 minutes. Add chicken, tomato, and stock. Bring to a boil, reduce heat, and simmer for 20 minutes. Add apple and cook 15 minutes longer. Add peas a few minutes before cooking is completed. Serve on rice.

Serves 4.

EASY MEXICAN MOLE FOR SIX

    2 3½-pound chickens, cut into serving pieces
    2 medium onions, chopped
    1 teaspoon salt
    ½ cup olive oil
    4 garlic cloves
    2 green peppers, chopped
    2 tablespoons sesame seeds
    ¼ cup bread crumbs
    6 tomatoes, peeled and chopped
    ½ cup chopped almonds
    ½ teaspoon chili powder
    3 tablespoons peanut butter
    ¼ teaspoon cinnamon
    2 ounces unsweetened chocolate, grated
    ½ cup Kahlúa
      salt and pepper

Place chicken pieces and onions in pot and cover with water. Bring to a boil, then add salt. Reduce heat to a simmer, cover, and cook for ½ hour. Transfer chicken to large dish and cool. Reserve 1 cup chicken stock. Pat cooled chicken dry and gently brown in ¼ cup heated olive oil, a few pieces at a time. Transfer browned chicken to heavy casserole or pot. Place remaining ¼ cup olive oil, garlic, green peppers, sesame seeds, bread crumbs, tomatoes, and almonds in blender and puree. Pour mixture over chicken in pot. Add chili powder, peanut butter, cinnamon, grated chocolate, Kahlúa, and reserved cup of chicken stock. Blend together, cover, and simmer for approximately 1½ hours, turning chicken occasionally. Adjust seasoning with salt and pepper.

HAWAIIAN CHICKEN

1 3½-pound chicken, cut into serving pieces
1 cup pineapple juice
1 cup soy sauce
1 teaspoon ginger
2 garlic cloves, crushed
3 tablespoons oil, or as needed
1 cup chunk pineapple

Mix pineapple juice, soy sauce, ginger, and garlic in large bowl and marinate chicken for at least 2 hours. Turn at least once. Heat oil and brown chicken a few pieces at a time, reserve marinade. When all chicken has browned, transfer to casserole. Add pineapple to marinade and pour over chicken, cover, and cook in preheated 350°F. oven for an hour. Turn chicken twice during cooking. Accompany with rice.

Serves 4.

INDIAN CHICKEN AND RICE

   1   3½-pound chicken, cut into 8 serving pieces
   1   stick butter
   1   tablespoon oil
  ½   cup flour
1½   teaspoons ground ginger
  ½   teaspoon ground mace
  2   teaspoons turmeric
  ½   teaspoon salt
  1   cup rice
  4   medium onions, sliced very thin
       oil for deep fat frying
  2   hard-boiled eggs
  ½   cup raisins
  ¼   cup pine nuts, toasted almond slivers or
       pistachio nuts

In large skillet melt 4 tablespoons butter and add oil. Combine flour, ginger, mace, ½ teaspoon only of turmeric, and salt. Coat chicken in spiced flour and fry in butter and oil for 15 minutes on each side or until done. Heat should be medium low. Meanwhile, cook rice according to package instructions, adding 1½ teaspoons turmeric. Deep-fat fry thinly sliced onions until golden. Drain. Melt 4 tablespoons remaining butter and stir into cooked rice. Add chicken and half of fried onions to rice and combine. Turn into serving dish. Garnish with a border of hard-boiled egg wedges and pile other half of fried onions in center of dish surrounded by raisins and nuts.

Serves 4.

ITALIAN BAKED CHICKEN

8 to 12 serving pieces of chicken
1 bottle Italian dressing (8 ounces)
   bread crumbs

Pour bottle of Italian dressing in bowl and coat each piece of chicken (better if you can marinate it overnight in the refrigerator). Roll each piece in bread crumbs and bake in buttered baking dish for 50 minutes to 1 hour in preheated 350°F. oven.

Serves 4 to 6.

MEXICAN CHICKEN

8 serving pieces chicken
   salt and pepper
½ cup olive oil
1 large onion, chopped
2 garlic cloves, minced
1 tablespoon chili powder
½ cup uncooked rice
1½ cups chicken stock
1 cup chopped tomatoes
2 tablespoons sliced green stuffed olives

Heat oil in large skillet and brown seasoned chicken on all sides. Add onion, garlic, and chili powder. Cook for 5 minutes. Add rice and pour stock over chicken. Cover and simmer for 25 minutes. Add tomatoes and olives, gently combine, and continue cooking for 5 more minutes. Adjust seasoning.

Serves 4.

MOO GOO GAI PAN
(Chicken and Mushrooms)

2 large chicken breasts, skinned, boned and
    cut into small pieces
4 tablespoons peanut or vegetable oil
2 garlic cloves, chopped
2 or 3 slices fresh ginger root or
    ½ teaspoon ground ginger
salt and pepper
1 tablespoon cornstarch
¼ pound fresh mushrooms, sliced
1 package frozen snow pea pods, partially
    thawed
10 water chestnuts, thinly sliced
4 scallions, sliced
2 tablespoons soy sauce
1 cup chicken stock

Heat oil in large frying pan and brown garlic and
ginger root, then discard garlic and root pieces.
Sprinkle chicken with salt and pepper and cook for
3 or 4 minutes, stirring often, over fairly high heat.
Reduce heat, sprinkle cornstarch over chicken, and add
remaining ingredients. Simmer for 15 minutes, adjust
seasoning and serve with fluffy white rice.

Serves 4.

PAELLA

Paella, one of the best-known dishes of Spain, acquired its name from the pan in which it is traditionally cooked. A paella pan is large, round, made of metal, not very deep and has a handle on both sides. There are many recipes for paella, but this recipe includes the four basic ingredients: rice, saffron, chicken, and seafood.

- 1 3-pound chicken, cut into 8 serving pieces
- ⅓ cup olive oil
- 2 garlic cloves, peeled and crushed
- 2 medium onions, chopped
- 1 medium green pepper, chopped
- ½ teaspoon oregano
- 1 teaspoon saffron
- 1 tablespoon parsley, chopped
- 1 teaspoon salt
  fresh ground pepper
- 2 chorizos (Spanish hot garlic sausage), sliced
- 1 large tomato, peeled, seeded, and chopped
- 2½ cups rice, uncooked
- 6 cups boiling chicken stock
- 1 pound shrimp, shelled and deveined
- ½ cup fresh or frozen peas—if frozen, partially thawed
- 1 1½-pound lobster—cooked, meat cut into pieces, and claws reserved for decoration
- 10 to 12 mussels or clams
  pimiento strips for decoration

In large skillet or paella pan heat olive oil, and brown chicken on all sides. Add garlic, onions, and green pepper. Sprinkle oregano, saffron, parsley, salt and pepper over chicken and add chorizos. Simmer for 10 minutes. If using a skillet, transfer all ingredients from skillet to large heavy casserole. On top of stove, add tomato and rice. Stir gently and add stock and shrimp. Bring to a boil, reduce heat to a simmer and cook, covered, over medium-high heat for 20 minutes. If paella pan is used, at this point put it on lower shelf in preheated 400°F. oven for 20 minutes, uncovered. Add peas, lobster meat, and carefully blend into paella. Decorate top with lobster claws, mussels or clams, which have been steamed in a little seasoned water until their shells open, and pimento strips. Next, if casserole is used, simmer for 5 minutes more and serve in casserole: or, return paella pan to oven uncovered for 5 minutes more. Serve with green salad, crusty bread, and red wine.

Serves 6.

Place an empty plate on each side of the paella for bones and empty shells.

POLLO ALLA PIZZAIOLA

  1 3-pound chicken, cut into 8 serving pieces
 ⅓ cup olive oil
  2 garlic cloves, crushed
  2 cups canned tomatoes and juice
  2 tablespoons tomato paste
 ½ teaspoon marjoram
  1 bay leaf
    salt and pepper

Heat olive oil in large skillet and over high heat, quickly brown chicken on all sides. Add garlic, canned tomatoes, which should be mashed with the back of a fork or spoon, tomato paste, marjoram, bay leaf and season well with salt and pepper to taste. Bring to a boil, reduce heat, and simmer, covered, for ½ hour. Add a little chicken broth if tomato mixture becomes too thick.

Serves 4.

POLLO CASALINGA

4 chicken breasts—halved, breastbones removed
  salt and pepper
  oregano
3 tablespoons olive oil, or as needed
3 tablespoons tomato paste
1 cup Chianti wine
¾ cup chicken broth
8 slices mozzarella cheese, ⅛ inch thick
8 large onion slices, ⅛ inch thick
2 lemons, cut into slices ¼ inch thick—
  seeds removed
  fresh chopped parsley

Wash breasts and pat dry. Season lightly with salt, pepper, and oregano. Heat olive oil in large skillet and brown chicken pieces well on both sides, a few at a time, adding more olive oil if necessary. In saucepan blend tomato paste, Chianti, and chicken broth and bring to a boil. Simmer for a minute or two. Then in shallow baking dish arrange browned chicken breasts skin side up in dish, overlapping one another, and top each with a slice of cheese, onion, and lemon. Pour sauce over chicken. Place in preheated 425°F. oven and cook for 15 minutes. Reduce heat to 350°F. and continue cooking for 20 minutes longer or until chicken is tender. Sprinkle with fresh chopped parsley.

Serves 4.

POLLO PAGLIAROLI

    1 2½-pound chicken, cut into 8 serving pieces
    ½ cup wine vinegar
    2 tablespoons oil
    ⅓ cup grated Parmesan cheese
    2 garlic cloves, minced
    ½ teaspoon dried basil
    ½ teaspoon salt
      fresh grated pepper
      fresh chopped parsley

Wash chicken pieces and pat dry with paper towels. In deep bowl, combine wine vinegar, oil, grated Parmesan cheese, garlic, basil, salt and pepper. Marinate chicken in mixture for 30 minutes. Grease shallow baking pan and place chicken in pan. Bake in preheated 350°F. oven for ½ hour. Turn and baste generously with marinade. Continue cooking for ½ hour more until nicely browned. Garnish with fresh chopped parsley.

Serves 4.

ROMAN FRICASSEED CHICKEN

1 2½-pound chicken, cut into 8 serving pieces
   salt and pepper
3 tablespoons olive oil
¼ pound prosciutto ham, sliced and cut into
   thin strips
2 tomatoes, peeled and chopped
1 garlic clove, crushed
½ teaspoon marjoram
1 cup red wine
½ cup chicken stock

Brown seasoned chicken in heated olive oil on all sides. Add prosciutto, tomatoes, garlic, marjoram, red wine, and chicken broth. Bring to a boil, reduce heat, and cover. Simmer for 35 minutes. Adjust seasoning.

Serves 4.

CHICKEN THE VERSATILE: CASSEROLES AND STEWS

Many people feel that the main qualification of a successful dish is that it be covered with a rich gravy or sauce: casseroles and stews are the answer. Economically speaking, a casserole or stew on the menu once or twice a week is a must for the family budget. The recipes included here will probably be served, by request as well as by necessity, many times and they can be reheated with excellent results. A simmering casserole on the table is both attractive and enticing.

BLANQUETTE DE POULET

2½ pounds chicken breast, cut into
        1½-inch pieces
3 cups chicken stock
1 carrot, chopped
1 medium onion, chopped
1 stalk celery, chopped
1 turnip, chopped (optional)
2 leeks, cut in half
    bouquet garni of 1 bay leaf, pinch of thyme,
        4 sprigs parsley, 6 peppercorns
    salt and pepper to taste
½ pound mushrooms, sliced
20 small white onions—poached in water until
        just tender (keep warm until used)

SAUCE

     3 tablespoons butter
     3 tablespoons flour
  2½ cups chicken stock
     2 egg yolks
  ½ cup heavy cream

Place chicken in large ovenproof casserole and add chicken stock. Bring to a boil, reduce heat to a simmer, and skim. Add carrot, onion, celery, turnip, leeks, bouquet garni, and salt and pepper. Cover and simmer for 30 minutes. Transfer chicken to covered heated dish while preparing sauce. Strain liquid from cooked chicken and save 2½ cups. Melt butter in saucepan and add flour, stirring constantly. Slowly add chicken stock, whisking all the time. Lightly beat egg yolks and add heavy cream. Put a few tablespoons of hot sauce into cream mixture, then pour cream mixture into sauce. Add mushrooms, poached small onions, and chicken. Heat thoroughly but don't boil. Serve on white rice. Garnish with fresh chopped parsley.

Serves 4 to 6.

BROWN CHICKEN FRICASSEE

1 3½-to-4-pound chicken, cut into 8
  serving pieces
  salt and pepper
4 tablespoons butter
1 medium onion, sliced
2 cups chicken broth
2 carrots, peeled and sliced
½ cup celery, minced
1 bay leaf
¼ teaspoon thyme
½ cup heavy cream

Rinse chicken and dry with paper towels. Season
with salt and pepper. Melt butter in Dutch oven.
Brown chicken on all sides. Add onion and sauté for
5 minutes. Pour broth over chicken and add carrots,
celery, bay leaf, and thyme. Cover and simmer for 50
minutes or until chicken is tender. Transfer chicken
to heated platter. Pour heavy cream into sauce and
adjust seasoning. Heat thoroughly and gently pour
over chicken.

Serves 4.

BRUNSWICK STEW

- 1 3-pound chicken, cut into 8 serving pieces
  salt and pepper
- 3 tablespoons bacon drippings
- 1 large onion, chopped
- ½ cup chopped green pepper
- 2 cups canned tomatoes, chopped
- 2 cups water
- 1 tablespoon Worcestershire sauce
  good dash cayenne pepper
- 1 tablespoon fresh chopped parsley
- 1 package frozen lima beans
- 1 cup whole kernel corn
- 2 tablespoons flour

Season chicken with salt and pepper and brown evenly in hot bacon drippings. Add onion and green pepper and sauté for 5 minutes. Pour in tomatoes, water, and Worcestershire sauce. Bring to a boil, reduce heat, and simmer, covered, for 25 minutes. Add cayenne pepper, parsley, lima beans, and corn. Cook, covered, 25 minutes more. Mix flour with a little water and stir gently into stew, which should thicken slightly. Cook for 5 minutes.

Serves 4 to 6.

Serve with crusty bread.

CHICKEN À LA BOURGUIGNON

     8 serving pieces chicken
     3 slices bacon, diced
     4 tablespoons butter
    20 small white onions
    16 mushrooms, sliced
     2 cups red Burgundy wine
     2 cups beef stock
       bouquet garni made of 1 stalk celery—
          quartered, 1 leek—quartered, 3 sprigs
          parsley, branch of tarragon, 6 peppercorns,
          and 1 bay leaf
       salt and pepper

Poach bacon in boiling water for 5 minutes. Drain. Melt butter in heavy earthenware casserole and sauté onions and mushrooms for 5 minutes. Remove mushrooms and onions with slotted spoon and brown chicken in same butter, adding more if needed. Transfer chicken to side dish. Pour in red wine and bring to a boil, reduce to ½, and add 2 cups beef stock. Return to a boil and add bouquet garni. Replace chicken in pot, cover, and simmer for ½ hour. Add bacon, onions, and mushrooms. Re-cover and cook 30 minutes longer. Adjust seasoning. Discard bouquet garni. Arrange chicken and accompaniments on heated serving dish and pour sauce over chicken. Or, entire dish can be served from casserole it was cooked in.

Serves 4.

CHICKEN AND ARTICHOKE HEART CASSEROLE

4 chicken breasts, split
  paprika
  salt and pepper
4 ounces butter or 1 stick
½ pound mushrooms, quartered
3 tablespoons flour
1½ cups chicken broth
¼ cup sherry
1 package frozen artichoke hearts, thawed

Wash chicken pieces and pat dry. Season well with paprika, salt and pepper. Melt 2 ounces or ½ stick of butter in skillet and brown chicken. Transfer to casserole. Add remaining 2 ounces butter to skillet and sauté mushrooms for 5 minutes. Sprinkle flour over mushrooms and stir gently. Pour broth and sherry over mixture. Continue cooking for a minute or two. Arrange artichoke hearts around the chicken in casserole, then pour mushrooms and sauce over chicken. Cover and bake for 40 to 45 minutes in preheated 350°F. oven.

Serves 4.

CHICKEN AND CORN CASSEROLE

2½ cups cooked chicken, cubed
2 tablespoons vegetable oil
1 garlic clove, minced
1 medium onion, chopped
1 small green pepper, diced
1 medium tomato, chopped
1½ tablespoons flour
1½ cups chicken broth
2 cups kernel corn
⅓ cup shredded Swiss cheese
salt and pepper to taste
¼ cup bread crumbs

Heat oil in skillet and sauté garlic, onion, and green pepper for 5 minutes. Add tomato and cook about 3 minutes more. Sprinkle flour over mixture and stir in broth a little at a time. Blend in corn, chicken, and cheese. Season with salt and pepper. Transfer to greased casserole and sprinkle with bread crumbs. Bake at 350°F. for 40 to 45 minutes until top is golden.

Serves 4 to 6.

CHICKEN AND NOODLE CASSEROLE

2 cups chopped cooked chicken
6 tablespoons butter
1 medium onion, chopped
1 pound package egg noodles, cooked
    and drained
1 can cream of mushroom soup
1 cup light cream
1 8-ounce can small peas, drained
1 teaspoon Lawry's Seasoned Salt
2 tablespoons sherry
¼ cup dried bread crumbs

Melt 2 tablespoons butter and sauté onion until transparent. Put cooked noodles in large bowl, add 2 tablespoons butter, chicken, and onion and gently combine remaining ingredients (except for bread crumbs). Place mixture in buttered casserole and sprinkle bread crumbs over surface of casserole and dot with 2 tablespoons remaining butter. Place in a preheated 375°F. oven for 30 to 35 minutes until top turns golden.

Serves 4 to 6.

CHICKEN AND ORANGE
CASSEROLE

- 8 serving pieces chicken
- 1 cup flour
- 2 teaspoons salt
- ¼ teaspoon pepper
- 1 tablespoon paprika
- 3 tablespoons oil
- 1 tablespoon butter
- ¾ cup peeled and diced carrots
- ¼ cup diced fresh mushrooms
- ½ cup minced onions
- ¼ cup raisins
- 2 teaspoons brown sugar
- ¼ teaspoon ginger
- 1 cup orange juice
- ½ cup chicken broth

Wash chicken and shake off excess water. Combine flour, salt, pepper, and paprika and dredge chicken in mixture. Heat butter with oil and brown chicken on all sides. Transfer chicken to casserole with carrots, mushrooms, onions and raisins. Blend together brown sugar and ginger, then whisk into orange juice and chicken broth. Pour over chicken and bake in preheated 350°F. oven for 1 hour.

Serves 4.

CHICKEN AND SAUSAGE
IN BEER

8 serving pieces chicken
   salt and pepper
   flour
4 tablespoons oil, or as needed
2 large onions, sliced
8 small link sausages
1 pint beer or ale

Season chicken with salt and pepper. Dredge in flour and brown on all sides in 2 tablespoons heated oil in skillet. Transfer to casserole, add 2 tablespoons oil to skillet, and sauté onions until transparent. Cover chicken with onions in casserole and top with sausages. Pour beer or ale in skillet and bring to a boil, scraping up any small bits that remain in pan. Pour over sausages in casserole. Cover and cook in preheated 350°F. oven for 45 minutes. Uncover, raise heat to 425°F., and cook 10 minutes more.

Serves 4.

CHICKEN BRAISED IN BEER

1 3½-pound roasting chicken
salt and pepper
5 tablespoons butter
2 shallots, minced
¼ cup brandy
¼ cup quartered mushrooms
½ cup heavy cream
2 cups dark beer
1 tablespoon cornstarch
fresh chopped parsley

Season cavity of chicken with salt and pepper. Truss. Melt 3 tablespoons butter in ovenproof casserole and brown chicken on all sides. Add shallots and pour brandy over chicken. Heat and ignite and wait for flame to burn out. Add mushrooms, heavy cream, and beer. Bring to a boil, reduce heat to a simmer, cover, and cook for 1 hour. Transfer chicken to serving dish and carve into serving pieces and keep warm. Reduce sauce by boiling rapidly for 5 minutes. Check seasoning. Dissolve cornstarch in a little water and add to sauce, stirring constantly. Swirl in 2 remaining tablespoons butter and pour sauce over chicken. Garnish with fresh chopped parsley.

Serves 4.

CHICKEN DINNER
IN A CASSEROLE

1 3½-pound roasting chicken
  salt
4 tablespoons butter
½ cup dry white wine
8 small white onions
24 small potatoes
2 ripe firm tomatoes, peeled and quartered

Season chicken's body cavity with salt, and truss. Place in ovenproof casserole and baste with melted butter. Put in preheated 350°F. oven for 30 minutes, basting chicken often with butter. Add white wine, onions, and potatoes. Continue cooking for ½ hour longer or until chicken is tender. Five minutes before chicken is done add tomatoes.

Serves 4.

CHICKEN FRICASSEE

1 3½-to-4-pound chicken or fowl, cut into
    8 serving pieces
2 medium onions, chopped
2 carrots, sliced
    bouquet garni of 3 sprigs parsley, pinch of
    thyme, bay leaf, and 6 peppercorns
1 teaspoon salt
    pepper to taste
2 tablespoons butter
2 tablespoons flour
1 egg yolk
½ cup heavy cream
1 teaspoon lemon juice

Place chicken, onions, carrots, and bouquet garni in
ovenproof casserole or Dutch oven. Add enough water
to cover chicken and bring to a boil. Add salt and
pepper. Simmer for 1½ hours or until chicken is
tender. Transfer chicken to warmed dish and strain
chicken stock. Melt butter in saucepan and add flour,
stirring constantly. Cook for 3 or 4 minutes and slowly
pour in 1¾ cups chicken stock—always stirring. In
small bowl blend egg yolk and cream and add a little
hot sauce. Combine and pour slowly into sauce but
don't boil. Add lemon juice, blend, and pour over
chicken. Garnish with fresh chopped parsley.

Serves 4.

CHICKEN GUMBO

1 4½-to-5-pound stewing chicken, cut into
    serving pieces
  salt and pepper
3 tablespoons bacon drippings
4 cups chicken stock
3 tablespoons butter
1 medium-large onion, chopped
2 stalks celery, chopped
1 medium green pepper, chopped
½ pound fresh okra, cleaned and chopped, or
    1 package frozen sliced okra, thawed
2 cups canned tomatoes
1 cup water
1 teaspoon Worcestershire sauce
½ cup rice
1 teaspoon filé powder (optional)

Season chicken with salt and pepper and brown on
all sides in bacon drippings. Transfer to casserole. Add
chicken stock and bring to a boil. Lower heat and
simmer for 1½ hours or until tender. Drain and reserve
stock. Wash casserole and dry. Melt butter in casserole
and sauté onion, celery, and green pepper for 5
minutes. Add okra and tomatoes. Bring to a boil and
simmer. Meanwhile, remove meat from bones and cut
chicken into small pieces. Add meat to casserole with
3 cups reserved and strained stock, water, Worcestershire sauce, and rice. Bring to a boil, reduce heat and
simmed for ½ hour or until rice is tender. Blend filé
powder with a little water and stir into gumbo. Don't
boil. Adjust seasoning.

Serves 4 to 6.

CHICKEN JAMBALAYA

2 cups chopped cooked chicken
3 tablespoons butter
1 clove garlic, crushed
1 medium onion, chopped
1 cup uncooked rice
1 small green pepper, diced
2 cups canned tomatoes and juice
1 teaspoon salt
1 chicken bouillon cube
2 cups water
½ cup tomato juice
1 bay leaf

Melt butter in Dutch oven. Sauté garlic and onion for 5 minutes. Add rice and simmer for 5 minutes. Add remaining ingredients, bring to a boil, cover and simmer for 25 to 30 minutes until rice is tender.

Serves 4.

CHICKEN MACARONI CASSEROLE

2 cups cubed cooked chicken
2 cups uncooked elbow macaroni
3 tablespoon butter
1 medium onion, chopped
1 stalk celery, finely chopped
1 can cream of mushroom soup
1 can golden mushroom soup
½ pound fresh mushrooms, sliced
18 black olives, pitted and sliced
1 6-ounce package almond slivers

Cook macaroni according to package directions and drain. Melt butter; add chopped onions and sauté for 5 minutes. Place macaroni and onions in large casserole, add remaining ingredients except for almond slivers and gently combine. Sprinkle almonds on top of casserole and dot with butter. Put in preheated 350°F. oven for 35 to 40 minutes until golden on top.

Serves 4 to 6.

CHICKEN, MEATBALL, AND SHRIMP CASSEROLE

        3 chicken breasts, halved
        6 cups chicken stock
        3 carrots, scraped and chopped
        2 stalks celery, chopped
        2 medium onions, chopped
          pinch thyme
       ⅓ pound ground beef
       ⅓ pound ground veal
       ⅓ pound ground pork
        1 teaspoon Lawry's Seasoned Salt
        1 egg
        1 tablespoon minced onion
        4 tablespoons butter
     2½ tablespoons flour
        1 whole pimiento, minced
        1 pound shrimp, cleaned and boiled
        3 tablespoons sherry
          salt and pepper

Pour chicken stock in large saucepan and add chicken breasts, carrots, celery, onions, and thyme.

Bring to a boil, lower heat, and simmer for 20 minutes. Meanwhile, mix beef, veal, and pork, seasoned salt, egg, and minced onion. Make about 18 tiny meatballs. Transfer cooked chicken breasts to side dish and drop meatballs in simmering stock. Cook until done, about 10 to 12 minutes. Carefully remove meatballs and set aside. Strain remaining stock and reserve carrots. In clean saucepan melt butter, blend in flour and cook over low heat for a minute or so. Slowly pour in strained chicken stock and stir until sauce thickens and is smooth. Skin and bone chicken breasts and cut meat into bite-size pieces. Add to sauce, along with meatballs, cut-up carrots, pimiento, boiled shrimp, and sherry. Heat to a boil. Season with salt and pepper and serve on fluffy rice. (Can be made a day in advance.)

Serves 6.

CHICKEN RICE CASSEROLE

    8 serving pieces of chicken
    1 cup raw rice
    1 cup sliced onions
    2 cups canned whole tomatoes, chopped
 1½ cups chicken broth
    1 package frozen peas, partially thawed
    1 bay leaf
   ½ pound mushrooms, quartered
   ¼ teaspoon thyme
    1 cup red wine
      salt and pepper to taste

Combine ingredients in large casserole, cover, and bake in preheated 350°F. oven for 45 minutes. Remove lid and cook 15 minutes more.

Serves 4.

CHICKEN WITH LEMON

2 chickens, cut into serving pieces, or 16 pieces of chicken
  bouquet garni made of: 1 chopped stalk of celery, bay leaf, thyme, 4 sprigs parsley, and 6 peppercorns
1 large onion, quartered
32 small white onions
3 tablespoons butter
3 tablespoons flour
1 tablespoon lemon juice or to taste
1 tablespoon grated lemon rind
2 egg yolks
½ cup heavy cream

Place chicken pieces, bouquet garni, and onion in large casserole dish and cover with water. Bring to a boil on top of the stove, then cover and put in preheated 350°F. oven for 1 hour. Remove chicken and keep warm and covered. Strain chicken stock and put in clean saucepan. Reduce to about 2 cups. Meanwhile, slowly boil little white onions for 15 minutes or until tender. Mash flour and butter together until smooth and add to stock along with lemon juice and grated lemon rind. In small bowl beat egg yolks and gently blend with cream. Add a couple tablespoons of hot lemon sauce to egg yolk mixture and stir. Now pour into lemon sauce and simmer but don't boil. Season with salt and pepper. Drain onions and place around chicken. Pour sauce over chicken and sprinkle with chopped parsley.

Serves 8.

This recipe can easily be cut in half to serve 4.

EL PARADOR CHICKEN

Carlos Jacott's restaurant, El Parador, is a fine Mexican restaurant in New York City. The following two recipes —examples of the splendid food offered on El Parador's menu—were given to me by the owner.

> 1 3-pound chicken, cut into 8 serving pieces
> 1 cup olive oil
> 2 cloves garlic, crushed
> 1 teaspoon oregano
> 1 bay leaf, crumbled
> ½ teaspoon paprika
>   salt and pepper to taste
> ¼ teaspoon MSG (optional)
> ½ teaspoon minced fresh garlic
> 2 tablespoons wine vinegar
> ⅛ teaspoon Tabasco
>   flour for dredging
> 1 medium-large onion

In deep bowl put 3 tablespoons oil, crushed garlic, oregano, bay leaf, paprika, salt and pepper to taste, and MSG if desired. Combine, add chicken and turn until each piece is well coated. Cover and refrigerate overnight, turning pieces a few times.

In a small bowl combine 3 tablespoons oil, minced garlic, vinegar, Tabasco, and salt and pepper to taste. Whisk and set aside until ready to use. Remove chicken from refrigerator and dredge in flour one piece at a time. Heat remaining oil in large skillet (should be about ⅔ cup of oil left). Put in chicken, skin side down, and cook over medium heat until golden on both sides, about 12 to 15 minutes per side. Remove to heated ovenproof serving dish and keep warm in low oven. Cut onion into 4 thick slices, fry in skillet until brown on one side, then turn over, cover, and cook for 5 minutes. Beat vinegar mixture and strain over chicken. Place onion slices on chicken and serve hot.

Serves 4.

EL PARADOR'S CHICKEN MOLE

    1 3½-to-4-pound chicken, quartered
    ¼ cup olive oil
    1 tablespoon paprika
    1 bay leaf, crumbled
      salt and pepper to taste
    ¼ teaspoon oregano
      mole sauce—see below

Place chicken in bowl and add oil, paprika, bay leaf, salt, pepper, and oregano. Turn chicken in mixture until all pieces are well coated. Cover and refrigerate overnight, turning chicken a few times. Prepare mole sauce in casserole and place chicken in simmering mole sauce. Cover and cook for about 1 hour or until chicken is tender.

MOLE SAUCE

- ¼ cup peanut or vegetable oil
- 1 cup finely chopped onions
- ¼ cup chopped medium-hot long red peppers*
- 1 tablespoon chopped garlic
- ¼ cup finely chopped mushrooms
- ⅓ cup finely chopped green pepper
- 1½ ounces mole powder*
- 1 scant tablespoon flour
- 1 cup cold water
- ½ teaspoon oregano
- 2 bay leaves
- ¼ teaspoon MSG (optional)
- 1 6-ounce can tomato paste
- 2½ cups beef broth
- ½ ounce Mexican chocolate*
  (or bitter chocolate)
  salt to taste
- ½ tablespoon cornstarch (optional)

Heat oil in a large casserole. Add onions, red pepper, garlic, mushrooms, and green pepper. Cook, stirring often, until onions are golden brown. Combine mole powder with flour and stir it into casserole. Still stirring, add water, oregano, bay leaves, MSG, tomato paste, broth, and chocolate. Stir until chocolate is dissolved. Simmer for about 2 hours. Season with salt

* These ingredients are available at Casa Moneo, 218 W. 14th Street in New York City, or at Mexican food specialty shops.

to taste. Dissolve cornstarch in a little broth and stir into sauce.

Serves 4.

GOUGÈRE DE POULET

Gougère, according to Larousse Gastronomique, *is a Burgundian pastry. It is a pastry similar to choux paste (cream puff pastry) with diced cheese incorporated. The dish below, with it's puffed collar, provides a treat that is both different and lovely to behold.*

```
1 3-to-3½-pound chicken
  bouquet garni: 1 bay leaf, pinch thyme,
    4 peppercorns, garlic clove
2 stalks celery, chopped
½ teaspoon salt
2 tablespoons butter
1 medium onion, sliced
¼ pound mushrooms, sliced
2 large carrots, scraped and thinly sliced
1½ tablespoons flour
1 cup chicken stock
1 tablespoon parsley
⅛ teaspoon thyme
2 tablespoons sherry
  salt and pepper to taste
```

Place chicken with giblets in pot with bouquet garni, celery, and ½ teaspoon salt. Cover with water and bring to a boil. Reduce heat and simmer for 1 hour. Transfer chicken to dish and cool. Strain stock and reserve 1 cup for recipe. When chicken has cooled slightly remove skin and bones. Cut chicken into small pieces and set aside. Melt butter and sauté onion for 3 minutes. Add mushrooms and carrots and cook 5 minutes. Sprinkle flour over mixture, stirring. Pour in stock and add parsley, thyme, and sherry. Bring to a boil, add chicken, and simmer for 5 minutes. Season to taste and turn off heat. Prepare choux paste.

CHOUX PASTE

- ½ cup water
- 4 tablespoons butter
- ½ cup flour
- 2 eggs
- ½ cup diced Cheddar cheese

Bring water to a boil and add butter. Remove from heat and add flour quickly, then stir vigorously over low heat for 15 to 20 seconds only, until mixture falls from side of pan and forms a ball around spoon. Cool and beat in eggs thoroughly one at a time. Fold in cheese. Place chicken mixture in buttered, low baking dish. Spoon choux paste evenly around border of chicken mixture and place in preheated 375°F. oven for about 35 to 40 minutes until golden brown. Be sure pastry is golden and firm or it will fall when taken out of the oven.

Serves 4.

ONION PEACH CHICKEN

8 serving pieces chicken
1 stick butter or 4 ounces
1 tablespoon soy sauce
⅔ cup peach juice
1 package dried onion soup mix

In small saucepan combine butter, soy sauce, and peach juice. Bring to a boil and remove from heat. Place chicken in baking dish and brush with ½ butter mixture. Sprinkle with onion soup mix, cover with lid or foil, and bake in preheated 400°F. oven for 30 minutes. Uncover, baste with remaining butter mixture, and bake 30 minutes more at 350°F.

Serves 4.

PIQUANT CHICKEN CASSEROLE

1 3-pound chicken, cut into 8 serving pieces
6 tablespoons butter
2 medium onions, sliced thin
½ pound mushrooms, sliced
1 tablespoon tarragon
1 tablespoon parsley
1 tablespoon lemon juice
salt and pepper to taste
½ cup dry sherry

Melt 4 tablespoons butter in large skillet and brown chicken on all sides. Transfer chicken to ovenproof casserole. Add 2 more tablespoons butter to skillet and sauté onions until transparent. Add mushrooms

and gently stir. Cook for 5 minutes, then sprinkle with
tarragon, parsley, and lemon juice. Season with salt
and pepper. Spoon mixture over chicken and pour in
sherry. Cover and cook in preheated 350°F. oven for
35 to 40 minutes.

Serves 4.

POTENT CHICKEN CASSEROLE
(On Top of the Stove)

        8 serving pieces chicken
        3 tablespoons butter
        ½ cup brandy
        1 tablespoon tomato paste
        1 tablespoon Bovril
    1½ tablespoons flour
        ½ cup dry white wine
        2 cups chicken broth
            salt and pepper
        2 tablespoons olive oil
        2 garlic cloves, quartered
        2 tablespoons diced green peppers
        8 mushrooms, sliced
        1 teaspoon lemon juice

Brown chicken in butter evenly. In separate pan
heat brandy, ignite and pour over chicken in skillet.
Add tomato paste, Bovril, and sprinkle flour over
chicken. Turn each piece of chicken and stir paste and
Bovril in gently. Pour in wine and broth. Bring to a
boil, reduce heat and simmer, covered, for 25 minutes.
Meanwhile, sauté garlic in olive oil for 4 or 5 minutes.
Discard garlic cloves and add green pepper, mush-

rooms, and lemon juice. Cook over medium heat for 5 minutes and pour over cooking chicken. Cover and simmer for 10 more minutes.

Serves 4.

POULE AU POT
(Chicken in the Pot)

1 4-pound chicken
1 medium onion
  bouquet garni made of: 1 bay leaf, pinch of
    thyme, 4 sprigs parsley, and 6 peppercorns
6 large carrots, peeled and quartered
5 stalks celery, quartered
6 leeks, cut in half
6 small white onions
  salt and pepper

Place peeled onion in cavity of chicken, sew up opening, and truss. Put chicken in a large casserole and add cool water to just cover chicken. Bring to a boil, skim, and add bouquet garni. Reduce heat to a simmer and cook for 30 minutes. Season with salt and pepper, add vegetables, and bring to a boil again. Reduce heat to a simmer, cover, and cook for about 30 minutes more or until chicken and vegetables are tender. Remove chicken to serving dish and surround with vegetables. Discard bouquet garni.

Serves 4.

POULET MARENGO

This dish was named after the Battle of Marengo in which Napoleon was the victor. After a long day of battle, the hungry emperor ordered his chef to prepare a celebration dinner. Using the only ingredients available, his inventive chef, Dunard, created Poulet Marengo. The classic garnishes for this dish are crayfish and fried egg yolks.

    1 3-pound chicken, cut into 8 serving pieces
    3 tablespoons olive oil
       salt and pepper
    4 shallots, minced
    1 garlic clove, crushed
    1 tablespoon flour
    1 cup dry white wine
    ½ cup chicken stock
    ½ teaspoon thyme
    1 bay leaf
   16 small white onions, peeled and left whole
    5 tablespoons butter
    2 teaspoons sugar
    ¼ pound mushrooms, sliced
    2 cups canned tomatoes
       fresh chopped parsley

In heavy earthenware casserole heat oil and brown chicken, seasoned with salt and pepper, on all sides. Add shallots and garlic and cook for 4 or 5 minutes. Sprinkle flour over chicken and turn each piece. Add wine, chicken stock, thyme, and bay leaf. Cover and simmer. Meanwhile, melt 3 tablespoons of butter in medium skillet and add onions. Sprinkle with sugar and cook until golden and a glaze forms, shaking pan

often. Transfer onions to plate and clean skillet. Melt
2 remaining tablespoons butter, add sliced mushrooms,
and sauté for 3 or 4 minutes, stirring gently. Remove
and add to simmering chicken, along with onions and
tomatoes. Recover and simmer 20 minutes longer.
Adjust seasoning. Sprinkle with fresh chopped parsley.

Serves 4.

SAVORY CHICKEN CASSEROLE

8 serving pieces chicken
3 tablespoons butter
2 garlic cloves, crushed
1 can cream of mushroom soup
1 cup white wine
½ teaspoon basil
¼ teaspoon dried savory
  salt and pepper to taste

Heat butter in skillet and brown chicken pieces on
all sides with garlic. Meanwhile, combine mushroom
soup, wine, basil, savory, salt and pepper in small
saucepan and bring to a boil. Arrange chicken in
casserole and pour mushroom soup mixture over
chicken. Cover and bake in preheated 325°F. oven for
1 hour. Remove cover for last 10 minutes of cooking.

Serves 4.

CHICKEN THE VERSATILE: DIETER'S DELIGHT

Low in calories but high in protein and other important nutrients, chicken is ideal for weight watching. With the help of marinades, citrus fruits, herbs and spices, one can still prepare a delectable meal. Serve chicken and feast with caloric abandon.

BOILED OR POACHED CHICKEN

- 1 4½-to-5-pound chicken
- ½ lemon
- 2 quarts mild chicken stock or water enough to cover chicken
- 1 medium Bermuda onion, stuck with 3 or 4 cloves
- 1 bay leaf
- 2 stalks celery, coarsely chopped
- 2 carrots, coarsely chopped
- 3 sprigs parsley

Truss chicken and rub all over with lemon half. Place in deep pot and cover with chicken stock or water. Add remaining ingredients. If water is used, also add 1½ teaspoons salt. Bring to a boil and cook for 3 or 4 minutes. Skim, cover, and reduce heat to a simmer. Cook for about 2 hours. Drain and remove trussing strings. Place on heated serving dish. If you're not on a diet cover chicken with rich cream sauce. I like Hollandaise or velouté.

Serves 4 to 5.

DEVILED CHICKEN

        1 2-pound broiling chicken—split in half,
             backbone removed
          salt and pepper
        3 tablespoons melted butter
     1½ tablespoons Dijon mustard
       ¼ cup dry bread crumbs

Flatten chicken slightly with cleaver and season with salt and pepper. Brush with butter and broil for 10 minutes on each side under medium broiler. Spread mustard over skin side of chicken and sprinkle with bread crumbs and 2 tablespoons melted butter. Broil until bread crumbs are golden brown.

Serves 2.

Double this recipe for 4 servings.

DIET BREAST OF CHICKEN WITH LEMON AND TARRAGON

        2 large chicken breasts, skinned, boned,
             and halved
        2 tablespoons sherry
        1 medium onion, chopped
       ½ cup chicken broth
        1 tablespoon lemon juice
       ½ teaspoon dried tarragon
          salt and pepper to taste
        2 tablespoons bread crumbs
        1 tablespoon Parmesan cheese

Place chicken breasts in 3 cups of water in a sauce-pan, add sherry and onion. Bring to a boil. Reduce heat to a simmer and cook for 20 minutes. Drain. Place in small greased baking dish. Blend broth, lemon juice, tarragon, salt and pepper and pour into baking dish. Sprinkle chicken with combination of bread crumbs and Parmesan cheese and place under broiler until golden.

Serves 4.

LIME CHICKEN

2 broiler chickens—cut in half and
    backbones removed
½ cup vegetable oil
½ cup lime juice
1 large onion, finely chopped
1 teaspoon tarragon
⅛ teaspoon cayenne pepper
   salt and pepper to taste

Place chicken in large dish with high sides. In bowl, mix remaining ingredients and pour over chicken. Refrigerate overnight. Turn chicken a few times. Place chicken on rack skin side down. Broil under medium heat, turning and basting with marinade every 5 to 8 minutes until chicken is nicely browned but not burned.

Serves 4.

SEASONED BROILED CHICKEN

2 small broilers about 2 pounds each—halved,
    backbones removed
2 lemon halves
    Lawry's Seasoned Salt
    butter, or polyunsaturated margarine

Rub chicken with lemon and sprinkle Lawry's
Seasoned Salt on both sides of chicken halves. Place on
grill rack bone side up and broil for about 20 minutes,
turning often. Baste with butter occasionally. This is
a fast and simple dinner. Lawry's Seasoned Salt can
be replaced with Beau Monde seasoning. Served with
a green vegetable and favorite salad this meal is very
good for most dieters.

Serves 4.

WAISTLINE WATCHERS' CHICKEN

1 2½-pound broiler—split in half, backbone
    removed
2 tablespoons polyunsaturated margarine
    paprika

Baste both sides of chicken with margarine and
sprinkle with paprika. Broil chicken, skin side down,
8 inches away from heat for 10 minutes. Turn and broil
12 to 15 minutes longer or until done.

Serves 2.

CHICKEN THE VERSATILE: LEFTOVER SPECIALTIES

Many a tasty dish can be made from leftover chicken or turkey as the recipes that follow indicate. Some, in fact, are so good that cooks will find themselves preparing a whole bird solely to be able to serve these special dishes. Turkey may be substituted in any of the recipes for pre-cooked or leftover meat. Though the initial investment may seem expensive, turkey is an economical buy because it will provide the family with several inviting meals.

AUSTRIAN CHICKEN FRITTERS

    2 cups finely minced cooked chicken
      salt and pepper
      pinch nutmeg
    1 tablespoon chopped parsley
    ⅓ cup heavy cream
    1 egg yolk
    8 slices white bread, crusts removed
    1 cup milk
    2 whole eggs
    ½ teaspoon Lawry's Seasoned Salt
    1 cup fine dried bread crumbs, or as needed
    4 tablespoons butter
    4 tablespoons oil

Combine minced chicken, salt and white pepper to taste, nutmeg, and parsley. Blend in heavy cream and egg yolk, then mix until easy to spread. Spread equal portions on 4 slices of bread. Top with a slice of bread to make a sandwich. Now mix together milk, two beaten eggs, and Lawry's Seasoned Salt. Carefully coat sandwiches lightly by dipping them in this mixture. Roll in bread-crumbs and fry in 4 tablespoons each of butter and oil until golden on each side. Add equal amounts of butter and oil as needed.

Serves 4.

BAKED CHICKEN RING

   3 cups finely chopped cooked chicken
   2 cups heated light cream
   2 eggs, lightly beaten
   1 cup bread crumbs
   ½ teaspoon paprika
   ½ teaspoon salt
      pepper to taste
   1 teaspoon Worcestershire sauce
   ½ cup chopped celery
   1 green pepper, chopped
   1 tablespoon lemon juice

Slowly pour hot cream over eggs, always stirring. Add remaining ingredients and blend well. Turn into greased mold. Bake in preheated 300°F. oven for 45 to 50 minutes until set. Let rest for 10 minutes before unmolding. Serve with a tempting sauce such as Mornay or curried Béchamel.

Serves 6.

CHEESE CRÊPES WITH CHICKEN AND HAM

CRÊPES

- ½ cup flour
- ¼ teaspoon salt
- 1 tablespoon oil
- 2 eggs
- 1 cup milk plus 2 tablespoons water
- ¼ cup grated Gruyère or Cheddar cheese

FILLING

- 2½ tablespoons butter
- 2 tablespoons flour
- 1 cup milk
- salt and pepper
- pinch cayenne pepper
- ½ cup cooked shredded chicken
- ½ cup shredded ham

GARNISH

- ¼ cup grated Gruyère or Cheddar cheese
- butter
- fresh chopped parsley

First, prepare crêpes. Mix flour, salt, oil, and eggs. Slowly beat in milk and water. Add grated cheese and refrigerate for a least 30 minutes. If batter is too thick add a little water.

For filling, melt butter, blend in flour and slowly pour in milk, whisking all the time. Season well with salt and pepper. When thick and smooth, add cayenne pepper, chicken, and ham.

Pour about ¼ cup crêpe batter into hot, well-oiled 6-to-7½-inch crêpe pan or skillet. Cook crêpes on both sides quickly until brown. Spread each with filling and roll up. Place in buttered shallow baking dish. Dot with butter and sprinkle with ¼ cup grated cheese. Put in preheated 400°F. oven until crêpes are golden and bubbling. Garnish with fresh chopped parsley.

Serves 4.

CHICKEN À LA KING

    2 cups cooked chicken, cubed
    5 tablespoons butter
    3 tablespoons flour
    1 cup light cream
    1 cup chicken stock
      salt and pepper
    1 small green pepper, diced
    8 mushrooms, sliced
    2 pimientos, diced

Melt 3 tablespoons butter and blend with flour over low heat until smooth. Add cream and chicken stock. Bring to a boil, reduce heat and simmer until smooth and thickened. Stir constantly. Season. In skillet, heat remaining 2 tablespoons butter and sauté green pepper and mushrooms for 5 to 8 minutes. Add to sauce along with chicken and pimientos. Heat thoroughly. Serve in pastry shells or on biscuits.

Serves 4.

CHICKEN AND CHIPPED BEEF CASSEROLE

1 cup cubed cooked chicken
4 tablespoons butter
1 medium onion, chopped
2 tablespoons finely chopped green pepper
1 cup dried beef, shredded
1½ tablespoons flour
1 cup light cream
   salt and pepper to taste
2 eggs, beaten
¼ cup dried bread crumbs
1 teaspoon fresh chopped parsley

Melt 2 tablespoons butter in saucepan and sauté onion and green pepper for 5 minutes. Add chicken and dried beef. Sprinkle with flour and stir. Slowly pour cream into pan, stirring constantly. Bring to a boil and season with salt and pepper. Take off heat and add eggs. Pour into greased casserole. Melt remaining 2 tablespoons butter, add bread crumbs and parsley, and sprinkle over top of casserole. Set casserole in pan of warm water. Bake about 40 to 45 minutes in preheated 350°F. oven.

Serves 4.

CHICKEN AND MUSHROOM
SPAGHETTI SAUCE

2 cups cubed cooked chicken
3 tablespoons olive oil
1 medium-large onion, chopped
2 garlic cloves, crushed
1 large can plum tomatoes—1-pound 12-ounce
    can
2 cans tomato sauce—8 ounces each
1 6-ounce can tomato paste
2 bay leaves
1 chicken bouillon cube
1 tablespoon fresh chopped parsley
    dash powdered rosemary
¼ teaspoon thyme
½ teaspoon oregano
½ pound fresh mushrooms, sliced
    fresh grated Parmesan cheese

Heat olive oil in heavy pot and sauté onion and garlic for 5 minutes. Add remaining ingredients (except Parmesan cheese), bring to a boil, reduce heat and simmer for 1 hour. Add a little water if too thick. Serve on cooked spaghetti, and sprinkle liberally with fresh grated Parmesan cheese.

Serves 4 to 6.

Delicious served with tossed green salad, Italian bread, and Chianti.

CHICKEN AND SHRIMP IN DILL SAUCE

- 2 cups cubed cooked chicken breast
- 2 tablespoons butter
- 2 tablespoons flour
- 1 teaspoon paprika
- ¾ cup milk, heated
- ⅔ cup heavy cream
- ¼ cup dry sherry
  salt and pepper to taste
- 1 cup cooked shrimp, halved
- 1 tablespoon finely chopped fresh dill

Melt butter in saucepan and stir in flour and paprika. Slowly pour in heated milk and cream, whisking constantly. Add sherry and salt and pepper to taste and simmer for 5 minutes. Add cooked shrimps and chicken. Continue simmering for 5 minutes. Sprinkle in dill and blend. Serve on fluffy white rice.

Serves 4.

CHICKEN AND SHRIMP NEWBERG

- 1½ cups cubed cooked chicken
- 1½ cups cooked deveined shrimp
- 4 tablespoons butter
- 2 tablespoons minced onions
- 2 tablespoons flour
- 2 cups light cream
- ½ teaspoon paprika
- 1 teaspoon lemon juice
- 1 teaspoon salt
- ¼ cup sherry
- 3 egg yolks

Melt butter and sauté onion for 3 or 4 minutes until transparent. Place in top of double boiler over pan of simmering water. Stir in flour and cook slowly for a few minutes. Add 1½ cups cream a little at a time, always stirring, until sauce is smooth, thick, and near boiling point. Add chicken, shrimp, paprika, lemon juice, salt, and sherry and heat thoroughly. Beat egg yolks and blend with remaining ½ cup cream. Stir into simmering mixture but don't boil. Serve on toast points and garnish with fresh chopped parsley.

Serves 4 to 6.

CHICKEN CROQUETTES

    3 cups ground cooked chicken
    2 tablespoons butter
    2 tablespoons flour
      dash paprika
    ¼ teaspoon salt
      dash pepper
    1 cup milk
    1 tablespoon minced onion
    1 teaspoon lemon juice
    1 tablespoon finely chopped parsley
    1 egg yolk
    ½ teaspoon salt
    ¼ teaspoon pepper
    1 whole egg
    1 tablespoon water
      fine bread crumbs
      oil for deep-fat frying

Melt butter and add flour, paprika, ¼ teaspoon salt and dash pepper. Blend until smooth and slowly pour in milk, constantly stirring until smooth and thickened. Cool. Combine sauce, onion, ground chicken, lemon juice, chopped parsley, egg yolk, ½ teaspoon salt, and ¼ teaspoon pepper. Refrigerate for 1 hour or more. Divide mixture into 8 portions and shape into cones or cylinders. Roll in bread crumbs. Combine whole egg and water and dip croquettes in mixture and roll in bread crumbs again. Deep-fat fry until golden all over.

Serves 4.

CHICKEN FRITTATA

Frittata, the Italian version of the omelet, offers a pleasant change for brunch or midnight supper menus. While the omelet is cooked only on one side and folded, the frittata is cooked on both before serving. Ingredients may vary—it is an excellent way to use leftover vegetables and meat.

    ½ cup cooked diced chicken
    7 tablespoons olive oil, or as needed
    1 heaping tablespoon minced scallions
    ½ cup diced zucchini
    1 sweet Italian sausage link, crumbled
    ½ cup green peas
    1 small tomato, peeled, seeded, and finely
        chopped
    1 clove garlic
    6 large eggs
    ¼ cup Parmesan cheese
      salt and pepper to taste

In skillet heat 1 tablespoon olive oil and sauté minced scallions, zucchini, and crumbled sausage for 5 minutes or until sausage is cooked. Transfer to bowl and add peas, tomato, and chicken. Gently combine. In 9-to-10-inch omelet pan heat 4 tablespoons olive oil and push garlic around in pan for a minute while oil is heating. Remove garlic and discard. Tip pan and coat sides of pan with oil.

In large bowl, beat eggs lightly, add Parmesan cheese, and salt and pepper to taste. Pour eggs into pan and stir a few times. Add chicken mixture. With spatula lift edges of frittata gently to allow uncooked egg to run underneath; shaking pan back and forth. Add more oil to side of pan if necessary. Frittata should always be able to slide. When eggs are just set, remove from heat and carefully pour off oil. Cover pan with a flat lid or cookie sheet and turn frittata over onto it. Quickly add 2 tablespoons oil to pan and slide frittata back into pan. Cook for only ½ minute and slide frittata out onto serving plate. Cut into wedges and serve hot or cold.

Serves 4 to 6.

CHICKEN LIVER RISOTTO

½ pound chicken livers, finely chopped
1 medium-large onion, chopped fine
8 tablespoons butter
¼ cup fresh minced mushrooms
1 whole pimiento, minced
salt and pepper
1 cup long grain rice
2 cups chicken stock, heated
¼ cup dry sherry
Parmesan cheese

Melt butter in skillet and sauté onion until limp. Add chicken livers and stir until liver loses red color, then add mushrooms and pimiento. Season well with salt and pepper. Add rice and cook for 10 minutes, stirring frequently. Pour in chicken stock and sherry. Cover and cook until rice is tender, about 20 minutes. Sprinkle liberally with Parmesan cheese.

Serves 4 to 6.

CHICKEN POT PIE

2 cups chopped cooked chicken
½ cup cubed cooked carrots
¼ cup cooked green peas
¼ cup cooked chopped celery
1 tablespoon grated onion
1 can cream of mushroom soup
¾ cup milk
1 egg yolk
1 tablespoon fresh chopped parsley
1 package prepared biscuits

Combine ingredients except for biscuits. Transfer chicken mixture to greased baking dish and top with biscuits. Bake in preheated 375° F oven for 25 minutes until biscuits are golden.

Serves 4.

CHICKEN SOUFFLE

2 cups very finely minced cooked chicken breasts
3 tablespoons butter
2 tablespoons flour
1 cup light cream
  pinch nutmeg
4 eggs, separated
  salt and white pepper to taste

Melt butter in saucepan and stir in flour and cook for a minute or two. Pour in light cream, stirring constantly, and cook until sauce thickens. Add nutmeg and chicken. Mix egg yolks with a few tablespoons of hot sauce, then add to chicken mixture. Season with salt and pepper. Beat egg whites until stiff but not dry and carefully fold into mixture. Pour into buttered soufflé dish with collar and bake in preheated 350°F. oven for about 30 to 35 minutes.

Serves 4 to 6.

CHILLED CHICKEN SOUFFLE

2 cups finely minced cooked chicken
1 envelope gelatin
¼ cup chicken consommé
1 can cream of chicken soup, heated
1 tablespoon powdered curry
1 cup heavy cream, whipped
salt and pepper to taste

Combine gelatin with consommé in large bowl. Add hot chicken soup and stir until gelatin dissolves. Add curry and chicken. When cool, fold in whipped cream and correct seasoning. Pour into greased 1½-quart soufflé dish. Chill thoroughly.

Serves 4 to 6.

CREAMY CHICKEN HASH

3 cups cubed cooked chicken
½ cup white wine
4 tablespoons butter
1 medium onion, chopped
1 teaspoon finely chopped parsley
1 teaspoon flour
2 cups cubed boiled potatoes
½ cup heavy cream
salt and pepper

Put chicken in a bowl, pour wine over it, and cover. Refrigerate for several hours. Sauté onion and parsley in butter for 8 minutes, stirring often. Sprinkle in flour. Add chicken, potatoes, and heavy cream. Bring to a boil and simmer for 5 minutes. Season well with salt and pepper and serve on toast. Sprinkle with paprika.

Serves 4.

CREAMY CHICKEN ON WAFFLES

> 1½ to 2 cups coarsely chopped cooked chicken
> 2 tablespoons butter
> 2 tablespoons flour
> 1¾ cups milk
>   salt and pepper
> ½ cup heavy cream
> 1 pimiento, chopped
>   waffles—frozen or fresh

Melt butter and blend in flour. Cook over low heat for a minute or so. Pour milk slowly into mixture, whisking constantly until smooth. Season well with salt and pepper. Add chicken, cream, and pimiento. Heat thoroughly. Spread on hot waffles and garnish with fresh chopped parsley and crisp crumbled pieces of bacon.

Serves 4.

CURRIED CHICKEN POTS

3 cups cooked chicken, cut into small cubes
6 round hard rolls
1 cup cubed cooked ham
¼ cup minced scallions
1 cup diced tomato
½ cup minced celery
1 cup mayonnaise
1 tablespoon curry powder
1 tablespoon lemon juice
   paprika

Cut top off rolls and scoop out soft bread interior.
Set aside. Combine chicken, ham, scallions, tomato,
and celery. In small bowl mix together mayonnaise,
lemon juice, and curry powder. Mix ¾ cup curried
mayonnaise with chicken and ham mixture and fill
hollowed-out rolls, then replace top on roll. Spoon
about 1 tablespoon curried mayonnaise over roll and
sprinkle with paprika. Place each filled roll on bed of
lettuce.

Serves 6.

THE CZAR'S CHICKEN
RICE PIE

2 cups cooked chicken
1 stick butter or ¼ pound
1 large onion, thinly sliced
3½ cups cooked rice
1 tablespoon dill
1 teaspoon tarragon
1 teaspoon chopped chives
   salt and pepper to taste
4 hard-boiled eggs, sliced
1 crust pie pastry recipe

Melt 4 tablespoons butter in skillet and cook sliced onion until transparent and limp. Blend cooked rice and remaining 4 tablespoons melted butter with dill, tarragon, chives, and chicken. In baking dish spread ½ of onions on bottom, then ½ of rice mixture, and arrange ½ of sliced hard-boiled eggs on top. Repeat layers. Top with rolled pastry dough ⅛ inch thick; crimp edges and place in preheated 375°F. oven and bake for 30 to 35 minutes or until crust is nice and brown.

Serves 4.

GREEN PEPPERS STUFFED
WITH CHICKEN AND HAM

- 1 cup cooked chicken, minced
- 1 cup cooked ham, minced
- 4 green peppers (evenly shaped)
- 2 tablespoons butter
- 1 medium onion, minced
- 8 fresh mushrooms, minced
- ½ cup corn kernels
- 1 cup tomato sauce
  salt and pepper to taste

Carefully cut stems off green peppers and cut in half. Remove seeds. Drop in boiling water to cover for 10 seconds. Drain. Place side by side in greased baking dish. Melt butter in skillet and sauté onion for 5 minutes; add mushrooms, chicken, ham, corn kernels, and tomato sauce. Simmer for 3 minutes. Season with salt and pepper, then stuff pepper halves and bake in preheated 375°F. oven for 30 to 35 minutes, partially covered with foil.

Serves 4.

MACARONI CHICKEN AND
CHEESE BAKE

    1 cup cubed cooked chicken
    ½ pound macaroni
    2 tablespoons butter
    1 cup grated Cheddar cheese
    1 tomato, peeled and chopped
    1 tablespoon minced onion
    ½ cup evaporated milk
    1 cup milk
    ½ cup chicken broth
    1 egg, beaten
    ½ teaspoon paprika
    ½ teaspoon salt
      pepper to taste
      bread crumbs

Cook macaroni according to directions on package.
Drain and combine with butter, chicken, ham, cheese,
tomato, and minced onion. Blend evaporated milk,
milk, and chicken broth, then add to macaroni with
beaten egg, paprika, salt and pepper. Combine
thoroughly and turn into buttered baking dish.
Sprinkle bread crumbs on top and dot with butter.
Bake in preheated 375°F. oven until browned on top,
about 25 minutes.

Serves 6.

RISOTTO PRIMAVERA
CON POLLO

1 cup chopped cooked chicken
1 stick butter or ¼ pound
1 medium onion, finely chopped
2 shallots, minced
1 stalk celery, finely chopped
1 large carrot, finely chopped
1 cup raw rice
½ cup chopped mushrooms
1 cup dry white wine
1 cup beef broth
  salt and pepper to taste
  grated Parmesan cheese

In large skillet melt butter and cook onion, shallots, celery, and carrot for 5 minutes. Add rice, chicken, and mushrooms. Cook until rice is transparent, stirring often, about 8 minutes. Heat wine and stock; pour into rice and season lightly with salt and pepper. Cover and cook over low heat for about 20 minutes or until rice is tender. Sprinkle liberally with Parmesan cheese.

Serves 4.

CHICKEN A LUNCHEON LIFT: SALADS

Salads are always a joy to the eye and a fresh treat whether served as a luncheon dish, light summer meal, or part of a luscious buffet or picnic table. Because it combines so well with other foods, chicken offers endless possibilities for salad. Presentation is important, so use your prettiest bowls and be sure to keep the pepper mill close at hand.

CHICKEN AND APRICOT SALAD SUPREME

2 cups cubed cooked chicken
1 cup chopped apricots
½ cup diced water chestnuts
½ cup diced celery
2 tablespoons minced scallions
½ cup mayonnaise
3 tablespoons sour cream
1 tablespoon lemon juice
   salt to taste
   crisp lettuce leaves

Combine chicken, apricots, water chestnuts, celery, and scallions. In small mixing bowl blend mayonnaise, sour cream, lemon juice, and salt to taste. Pour over chicken mixture and gently toss. Serve on lettuce leaves.

Serves 4.

CHICKEN AND AVOCADO SALAD

    3 cups cubed cooked chicken
    2 avocados—peeled, pitted, and cut into
        1-inch cubes or balls
    4 strips of crisp cooked bacon, crumbled
    ½ cup chopped scallions
    ½ cup chopped celery
    2 tomatoes, peeled and cut into wedges
    ¼ cup lemon juice
    3 tablespoons vinegar
    ¼ cup olive oil
    ⅛ teaspoon cayenne pepper
       salt and pepper to taste
       crisp lettuce leaves

Combine all ingredients except for lettuce. Toss salad and serve on crisp lettuce leaves. Top with mayonnaise seasoned with parsley and a little lemon juice.

Serves 4 to 6.

CHICKEN AND BACON SALAD

    2 cups cooked diced chicken
    ½ cup crumbled crisp bacon
    1 cup diced tomatoes
    2 tablespoons sliced scallions
    ½ teaspoon dried basil
    1 tablespoon lemon juice
    ½ cup mayonnaise
       salt and pepper to taste

Combine ingredients and season with salt and pepper. Serve on bed of shredded lettuce or in sandwiches.

Serves 4.

CHICKEN AND CHESTNUT SALAD

2 cups diced cooked chicken
1 cup boiled chestnuts, chopped
¾ cup celery, diced
3 hard-boiled eggs—2 chopped and 1 sliced
8 stuffed olives, sliced
1 cup mayonnaise
   salt and pepper
   crisp lettuce leaves
   watercress
10 cherry tomatoes

Combine chicken, cooled chestnuts, celery, chopped eggs, olives, and mayonnaise. Season with salt and pepper. Arrange crisp lettuce leaves on serving dish and heap mixture into center. Surround with alternating watercress, tomatoes, and sliced egg.

Serves 4.

CHICKEN AND
MANDARIN ORANGES SALAD

2 cups diced cooked chicken
1 cup mandarin oranges
¼ cup diced water chestnuts
¾ cup diced celery
1 cup cooked white rice, cooled
  salt and pepper
½ cup mayonnaise
½ teaspoon curry powder
2 tablespoons mandarin orange juice from can

Place chicken, mandarin oranges, water chestnuts, celery, and rice in large bowl and gently toss. Season with salt and white pepper. In separate bowl combine mayonnaise, curry powder, and orange juice. Spoon over chicken mixture and carefully toss.

Serves 4.

CHICKEN AND WALNUT SALAD

2 cups cubed cooked chicken
2 tablespoons butter
½ cup walnuts
3 stalks celery, chopped
  lettuce
½ cup mayonnaise
2 tablespoons orange juice

Melt butter and brown walnuts. Cool and chop them coarsely. Combine with chicken and celery.

Arrange on lettuce leaves and top with mayonnaise blended with orange juice.

Serves 4.

CHICKEN CHUTNEY SALAD

2 cups diced cooked chicken
1 cup mayonnaise
½ cup chutney
1 tablespoon rum
¼ cup raisins
3 tablespoons roasted peanuts
¼ cup shredded coconut
2 bananas, sliced
   salt and pepper to taste
   lettuce leaves
2 tablespoons lemon juice
1 avocado pear, pitted and sliced

Combine mayonnaise, chutney, and rum. Add raisins, peanuts, coconut, bananas, and chicken, and gently toss. Pile mixture on lettuce leaves for individual servings. Coat avocado with lemon juice and garnish each serving with avocado slices.

Serves 4.

CHICKEN MAYONNAISE

4 chicken breasts, skinned, boned, and halved
  lettuce leaves
1 tablespoon oil
1 tablespoon vinegar
  salt and pepper
1 cup mayonnaise
4 hard-boiled eggs
2 tablespoons capers
8 anchovy fillets

Poach 8 pieces of chicken breast in seasoned water for 30 minutes. Trim into uniformly shaped ovals and arrange on top of crisp lettuce leaves on serving platter. Combine oil, vinegar, salt and pepper, then sprinkle over chicken. Coat each piece of chicken with mayonnaise and garnish with quartered hard-boiled eggs and capers. Carefully cut anchovies in half lengthwise and put 2 pieces of anchovy crisscrossed over each piece of chicken.

Serves 4 to 6.

CHICKEN WALDORF SALAD

2 cups cubed cooked chicken
2 cups diced unpared Delicious apples
1 cup chopped celery
¾ cup chopped walnuts
2 tablespoons apple juice
1 cup mayonnaise
½ teaspoon salt
  pepper to taste
  lettuce leaves

Combine chicken, apples, celery, and walnuts. Toss with apple juice, mayonnaise, salt and pepper. Serve on crisp lettuce leaves.

Serves 4 to 6.

CURRIED CHICKEN SALAD

2 cubed cooked chicken breasts—skins removed
2 ripe medium tomatoes
2 hard-boiled eggs, chopped
3 anchovy fillets—soak in milk to help remove
   saltiness, drain, and mince
1 medium head iceberg lettuce—break into
   small bite-size pieces
1 small red onion, minced
2 tablespoons minced green pepper

DRESSING

4 tablespoons oil
1½ tablespoons vinegar
1 teaspoon curry powder
   salt and pepper to taste

Cut tomatoes in half and squeeze out juice and seeds. Chop tomatoes and put in large salad bowl along with chicken, eggs, anchovy fillets, lettuce, onion, and green pepper. Mix dressing in separate bowl and pour over salad. Gently toss.

Serves 4 for light lunch or 6 for a side salad dish.

Sesame breadsticks are a nice accompaniment.

PEACHY CHICKEN SALAD

2 cups diced cooked chicken, light and
    dark meat
3 ripe medium-size peaches, pitted, peeled,
    and sliced
1 stalk celery, minced
8 water chestnuts, diced
1 small Spanish onion, minced
1 head iceberg lettuce, shredded

DRESSING

½ cup sour cream
3 tablespoons mayonnaise
1 tablespoon lemon juice or to taste
    salt and pepper

Put chicken, peaches, celery, water chestnuts, and onion in large bowl, and combine. Mix dressing in small bowl and dribble over chicken salad. Toss gently and serve on a bed of crisp shredded lettuce.

Serves 4 to 6.

PLAIN CHICKEN SALAD

3 cups cubed cooked chicken
1 cup chopped celery
¼ cup minced scallions
2 tablespoons minced green peppers
1 cup mayonnaise
½ teaspoon salt
    pepper to taste
1 tablespoon lemon juice
    crisp romaine, iceberg, or Boston lettuce

Combine chicken, celery, scallions, and green pepper. Blend mayonnaise, salt, pepper, and lemon juice. Toss with chicken mixture and pile on crisp lettuce. Garnish with tomato wedges, sliced hard-boiled eggs, or asparagus tips.

Serves 4 to 6.

POLYNESIAN CHICKEN SALAD

2 cups cubed cooked chicken
2 avocados, cut in half
3 tablespoons lemon juice
1 Delicious apple, peeled, cored, and diced
1 banana, quartered and sliced
1 orange—peeled, seeds and membranes
    removed, each orange segment cut in half
16 green grapes
½ cup pineapple chunks
2 tablespoons pineapple juice
¾ cup mayonnaise

Cut avocados in half and remove pits. Sprinkle with 1 tablespoon lemon juice. Combine remaining tablespoons of lemon juice with other ingredients and spoon into avocado halves.

Serves 4.

SZECHWAN SPICED
CHICKEN SALAD

2 large chicken breasts, halved
2 slices fresh ginger root
2 scallions, chopped
4 cups shredded lettuce
3 tablespoons peanut or vegetable oil
1 teaspoon minced ginger root
¼ teaspoon crushed chili pepper
¼ cup chopped scallions
2 garlic cloves, minced
2 tablespoons soy sauce
1 tablespoon dark Karo syrup

Bring 2 quarts of water to a boil with chicken breasts, 2 slices ginger root, and 2 chopped scallions. Reduce heat, cover, and simmer for 20 minutes. Remove from heat and allow chicken to cool in water. Skin and bone chicken. Shred chicken and blend with lettuce and set aside. Combine remaining ingredients and pour over chicken and lettuce. Gently toss and serve immediately.

Serves 4.

CHICKEN A LUNCHEON LIFT: SANDWICHES

Open-faced sandwiches, hot or cold, are particular luncheon favorites, but any sandwich can be a treat as long as it isn't too dry. The recipes included in this section avoid that particular sin and they offer an unusual array of combinations. For eye appeal and variety, use different kinds of bread, cut sandwiches in interesting shapes and tempting sizes, arrange them on plates with odd tidbits such as dilled beans or marinated mushrooms.

When making sandwiches for several people, use the assembly line method of adding the same ingredient to each sandwich at the same time. If butter or margarine is used it should be softened to room temperature. Keep a sharp knife handy for slicing and trimming crusts.

DAGWOOD CHICKEN SANDWICH

8 slices cooked chicken
8 slices rye bread
½ cup mayonnaise
8 strips crisp cooked bacon
4 thin slices Bermuda onion
8 bread and butter pickles
4 slices Swiss cheese
4 slices tomato
4 crisp lettuce leaves

Spread mayonnaise generously on each slice of bread. Top each of four slices of bread with the following: 2 slices chicken, 2 strips bacon, 1 slice Bermuda onion, 2 pickles, 1 slice Swiss cheese, 1 slice of tomato, and a lettuce leaf. Top each with slice of bread and cut in half.

Serves 4.

DENVER SANDWICH

8 generous slices cooked chicken breast or
    enough to serve 4*
4 English muffins
    butter
3 tablespoons butter
1 medium onion, thinly sliced
2 large carrots, scraped and grated
¼ pound fresh mushrooms, chopped
2 cups bean sprouts, drained
1 tablespoon soy sauce
2 medium tomatoes, cut into 4 slices each
8 ounces grated Cheddar cheese

Split English muffins in half and lightly toast. Spread with butter. Set aside. Melt 3 tablespoons butter and sauté sliced onion and grated carrots for about 5 minutes until onions are transparent. Add mushrooms and cook slowly for 5 minutes longer. Stir in bean sprouts, add soy sauce, and cook until evenly heated. Place chicken in equal portions on buttered toasted English muffins and spoon on bean sprout mixture. Top each with tomato slice and sprinkle with grated

* Turkey can be substituted for chicken

Cheddar cheese. Place under preheated broiler until
cheese turns golden brown. Serve immediately.

Serves 4.

CHICKEN AND PARSLEY
BUTTER SANDWICHES

8 slices cooked chicken breast
8 slices pumpernickel
2 ounces butter or 4 tablespoons
2 tablespoons finely chopped fresh parsley
4 thin slices Bermuda onion

Spread blended butter and parsley on each slice of
bread. Place 2 slices of chicken breast and 1 slice of
onion on each of 4 slices. Cover with other slices of
bread, cut into thirds, and garnish with watercress.

Serves 4.

CHOPPED CHICKEN LIVER
SANDWICHES

½ pound chicken livers
1 tablespoon sherry
2 hard-boiled eggs, chopped fine
6 strips crisp cooked bacon, crumbled
1 tablespoon lemon juice
2 drops Tabasco sauce
  salt and pepper to taste
1 medium onion, sliced thin

Put ½ cup water and sherry in saucepan and bring
to a boil. Add chicken livers and bring to a boil again.

Reduce heat and simmer for 10 minutes until livers are cooked. Drain, cool, then chop or mash livers until pulplike. Place in bowl and add chopped eggs, bacon, lemon juice, and Tabasco. Season with salt and pepper. Spread evenly on 4 slices of buttered bread. Top with thin slices of raw onion. Serve sandwiches open or cover with another slice of bread and cut each sandwich into 3 sections of equal proportions.

Serves 4.

CROQUE MADEMOISELLE

This is a variation on the Croque Monsieur and made exactly the same way except chicken is used instead of ham.

8 slices white sandwich bread, crusts trimmed off
8 thin slices Swiss cheese
4 thin slices chicken breast
    (cheese and chicken should be cut same size
    as the bread)
butter

Place 4 pieces of bread on counter and put a slice of cheese on each, top with a slice of chicken and another slice of cheese. Cover each with a slice of bread. Melt 3 tablespoons of butter in large skillet or grill. Sauté sandwiches by placing them in pan with a spatula. When golden on one side, remove, add more butter and sauté on other side until golden. Cut each croque in half diagonally or in 3 rectangles and serve on heated luncheon plates.

Serves 4.

MONTE CRISTO SANDWICH

4 **thin slices breast of cooked turkey or chicken**
8 **slices day-old white bread**
4 **thin slices ham**
4 **thin slices Swiss cheese**
2 **eggs, beaten with 1 tablespoon water**
4 **tablespoons butter or as needed**
   confectioners sugar
   maple syrup

Trim crusts from bread. Place turkey or chicken on 4 slices of bread. Top with slice each of cheese and ham and cover with remaining slices of bread. Dip each sandwich in beaten egg and water mixture. Sauté sandwiches in 2 tablespoons of butter until golden on each side. Add butter as needed. These sandwiches can be deep-fat fried in oil, but I prefer sautéing them in butter. Sprinkle each sandwich with confectioners sugar and cut diagonally into 4 triangles. Serve with maple or other syrup.

Serves 4.

NEW CHICKEN CLUB SANDWICHES

- 8 slices chicken (enough for 4 sandwich servings)
- 8 slices white bread
- ½ cup Russian Dressing
- 4 slices Munster cheese
- 8 slices tongue
- 4 slices tomatoes
- 4 crisp lettuce leaves
  salt and pepper

Spread Russian dressing on each slice of bread. Top 4 pieces of bread with 2 slices chicken, a slice of Munster cheese, 2 slices tongue, a slice of tomato, and a lettuce leaf. Season with salt and pepper and place bread on top. Cut each sandwich into 4 triangles.

Serves 4.

OPEN-FACED CHICKEN AND AVOCADO SANDWICHES

- 8 ⅛-inch-thick slices cooked chicken breast
- 4 slices black bread or pumpernickel
  butter
- 2 ripe avocados cut into twelve ½-inch-thick wedges
- ⅔ cup mayonnaise
- 2 tablespoons pineapple or peach juice
- 4 slices crisp cooked bacon, crumbled

Lightly butter each slice of bread. Place two slices of chicken breast on bread and top with 3 slices of avocado. Mix mayonnaise and pineapple or peach juice together and spoon flavored mayonnaise over avocado. Sprinkle bacon over mayonnaise.

Serves 4.

VIBRAPHONE SANDWICH

This unpretentious little sandwich was served in a gem of a restaurant called The Hip Bagel located in Greenwich Village in New York City. All their sandwiches were served on fresh bagels. A knife and fork are needed. Even though the shop is no longer with us, the recipe remains.

    4 bagels
    4 tablespoons butter
    ¾ cup cream cheese
    4 generous slices cooked breast of chicken
        or turkey
    4 slices boiled ham
    2 cups shredded lettuce
    8 slices of tomato
    1 medium red onion, thinly sliced
    ½ cup chopped walnuts
    ¾ cup maple syrup

Cut bagels in half and spread each half with ½ tablespoon butter. Toast under broiler until golden. Spread each with cream cheese and place 2 bagel halves on individual serving plates. Repeat following procedure for each sandwich: Place slice of chicken or turkey on one bagel half and ham on the other. Sprinkle ½ cup shredded lettuce across both halves.

Top with slice of tomato on each half. Break onion slice or two into rings and arrange across tomatoes. Combine walnuts and syrup and spoon approximately ¼ cup across sandwich.

Serves 4.

STUFFING

The savory aroma of an herb stuffing floating out from the kitchen is a sure sign of a holiday and the recipes that follow should prove worthy of a festive occasion. Flavorful stuffings can also provide a new and different casserole for a daily meal—just be sure to make them especially moist. Bake them in your favorite casserole dish in a moderate oven for about 25 minutes or until they are heated throughout and the top is crusty.

Though white bread is the most popular, stuffing can be made with wheat, rye, or almost any bread you choose. It is better to use one- or two-day-old bread so that it won't become pasty. Corn bread, rice, fruit, cabbage, and sauerkraut also make excellent stuffing. Since stuffing is highly perishable it should be made just before roasting the bird. Stuffing should always be light and moist, but never soggy. Some very tasty commercial stuffings are available in markets today. Additions can be made to these prepared stuffings by sautéing onions, or celery, nuts, mushrooms, sausages, and so on, and adding to the mixture that has been prepared according to the package directions.

STUFFING AND TRUSSING

The essential thing to remember when preparing the bird for roasting is not to pack the stuffing too tightly in the cavity because it will expand during cooking. Allow about ¾ cup of stuffing for each pound of bird. Spoon stuffing into the neck cavity first, lightly, then secure skin to back of bird with metal skewer. Sprinkle body cavity with salt, then stuff. Sew opening closed with string, or close by inserting skewers across opening and lacing with string. Tie legs together. Many frozen birds are already held together by a slit made in the skin—just place the legs back through the slit after the bird has been stuffed. Or see alternate method for trussing on page 13. Extra stuffing can be cooked separately in a greased baking dish until lightly brown on top.

ALMOND RICE STUFFING

1 cup cooked rice
1 rounded tablespoon raisins
1 small onion, minced
3 tablespoons fresh chopped parsley
4 ounces ground blanched almonds
    liver of chicken, minced
2 tablespoons butter, softened
1 egg, lightly beaten
    salt and pepper to taste

Mix all ingredients together well before stuffing bird.

Stuffing for 3½-to-4-pound roasting chicken.

ALMOND STUFFING

2 sticks butter or ½ pound, melted
1 large onion, chopped
3 stalks celery, chopped
1 teaspoon sage
1 teaspoon marjoram
½ teaspoon thyme
½ teaspoon savory
1 teaspoon salt or to taste
5 cups toasted whole wheat day-old bread cubes
5 cups toasted white day-old bread cubes
2 cups toasted slivered almonds

Melt 4 tablespoons butter and sauté onions and celery for 8 to 10 minutes until transparent. Transfer to large bowl and combine with remaining ingredients.

Makes about 8 cups of stuffing for 10-to-12-pound turkey.

BASIC TURKEY STUFFING

1 cup chopped onions
3 stalks celery, chopped
1 stick or 4 ounces butter, melted
8 cups day- or two-day-old bread cubes
    or crumbs
1 egg, lightly beaten
2 teaspoons poultry seasoning
¾ cup chicken broth
½ cup fresh chopped parsley
1 clove garlic, minced

Sauté onions and celery in butter until transparent. Place bread cubes or crumbs in large bowl and gently combine with onion and celery mixture. Add remaining ingredients. If you use packaged seasoned bread cubes, simply omit poultry seasoning in this recipe.

Makes about 8 cups stuffing for 10-to-12-pound bird.

CHESTNUT STUFFING

You will need about 4 pounds of chestnuts for this recipe. With a sharp knife make slit on flat side of chestnuts. Cover with water in saucepan and bring to a boil. Remove from heat. One at a time remove shells and inner skins of chestnuts. Cover peeled chestnuts with chicken stock and simmer for ½ hour or until chestnuts are just soft. Drain and chop. Canned whole chestnuts can be purchased in specialty shops if fresh chestnuts aren't available. They save time and taste quite good.

    1 stalk celery, minced
    1 medium onion, minced
  ½ cup butter
    1 pound bulk pork sausage
    4 pounds chestnuts, or 2½ cups chopped
        canned chestnuts
  ⅓ cup Cognac
    1 tablespoon fresh chopped parsley
  ½ teaspoon dried marjoram
    1 teaspoon salt
  ½ teaspoon freshly ground pepper
    3 cups toasted bread crumbs

Cook celery and onion in butter until slightly golden. Drain off butter and save. Add sausage and cook until no longer pink, stirring often. Pour off fat. In large bowl combine sausage, celery, onions, and butter with chestnuts, Cognac, parsley, marjoram, salt and pepper, and bread crumbs. Stir gently. Correct seasoning.

Makes 8 cups of stuffing for 10-to-12-pound turkey or goose.

CORN BREAD, PECAN, AND SAUSAGE STUFFING

      1 pound country sausage
      2 medium onions, chopped
      2 stalks celery
   1½ cups chopped pecans
   5½ cups crumbled corn bread
      2 tablespoons fresh chopped parsley
      ½ teaspoon dried basil
      1 teaspoon salt
         pepper to taste
      ⅓ cup sherry
      2 tablespoons water
      1 stick butter or ¼ pound melted butter

In large skillet cook sausage, breaking it apart with a fork and stirring until no pink color remains. Remove sausage with slotted spoon and drain in strainer. Pour off all fat from skillet except 2 tablespoons and sauté onion and celery for about 5 minutes, stirring often. Transfer to large bowl and add drained sausage and remaining ingredients. Blend well.

Stuffing for 12-to-14-pound bird.

CORN BREAD STUFFING

  2 cups white bread crumbs
  4 cups corn bread, crumbled
  ¾ cup chopped celery
  2 medium onions, finely chopped
1½ teaspoons salt
  ½ teaspoon poultry seasoning
  1 cup oysters, chopped (optional)
  ¾ cup melted butter
  3 hard-boiled eggs, chopped
  ½ teaspoon ground pepper
    rich chicken stock

Combine ingredients and add enough stock to moisten stuffing. Should not be soggy.

Stuffing for 8-to-10-pound turkey.

NOODLE STUFFING

    liver of bird
  8 tablespoons butter or ¼ pound
  2 medium onions, chopped
  3 cups cooked egg noodles
  ½ cup liver pâté, chopped
  ¼ cup fresh chopped parsley
  ½ teaspoon thyme
    salt and pepper to taste

Sauté liver in 2 tablespoons butter for a few minutes, turning. Cool slightly and chop fine. Sauté onion for

5 minutes in same butter. Add remaining butter; when melted gently fold in remaining ingredients.

Stuffing for 4-to-5-pound roasting chicken or duck.

HOLIDAY STUFFING

> 4 tablespoons butter
> 1 stalk celery, minced
> 1 medium onion, chopped
> ¼ teaspoon thyme
> ½ pound ground veal
> ½ pound pork sausage
> 1 cup cooked wild rice mixture
> 4 dried apricots, chopped
> 16 small fresh green grapes
> ¼ cup pignola nuts
> 4 slices prosciutto, chopped
> 6 small mushrooms, chopped
> ½ teaspoon sage
> 4 cups bread crumbs
>   salt and pepper to taste

Melt butter and sauté celery and onion with thyme for 5 minutes. Transfer to large mixing bowl. Sauté combined veal and sausage until no pink color remains. Drain. Add to large bowl with remaining ingredients and combine thoroughly.

Stuffing for an 8-to-10-pound turkey or capon.

OYSTER STUFFING

- 4 cups bread cubes
- ¼ teaspoon thyme
- ½ teaspoon sage
- ¼ teaspoon nutmeg
- 1 teaspoon salt
- 1 cup melted butter or 2 sticks
- 1 egg, beaten
- 2 cups oysters, chopped
- ½ cup white wine

Blend all dry ingredients in large bowl. Add remaining ingredients and mix well.

Stuffing for 9-to-10-pound turkey.

MUSHROOM STUFFING

- 1 pound mushrooms, chopped
- 1 cup chopped onions
- 1 tablespoon fresh chopped parsley
- 8 cups bread cubes
- 1½ sticks butter or 12 ounces
- 1 teaspoon salt

Melt butter in skillet and sauté mushrooms and onions for about 10 minutes, stirring often. Combine with parsley, bread cubes, salt and pepper and toss.

Stuffing for 10-to-12-pound turkey.

SHALLOT STUFFING

- 10 cups day-old bread cubes
- ¾ cup butter, melted
- 1½ cups minced shallots
- ¼ cup fresh chopped parsley
- 1 tablespoon tarragon
- ½ teaspoon minced garlic
- ½ teaspoon thyme
- 2 teaspoons salt
- ½ teaspoon fresh ground pepper
- ½ cup chicken broth
- 2 tablespoons brandy

Place bread cubes in large bowl and blend in butter, then add remaining ingredients.

Stuffing for 12-to-16-pound turkey.

SAUSAGE STUFFING WITH WHOLE WHEAT BREAD

- ½ stick butter or 2 ounces
- 2 medium onions, chopped
- 2 cups chopped celery
- 1 pound bulk country sausage, crumbled
- 1 tablespoon marjoram
- 8 cups day-or-two-old whole wheat bread crumbs
  salt and pepper to taste

Melt butter and sauté onions and celery until transparent. Transfer sautéed mixture with butter to large mixing bowl. Cook sausage until no pink color remains.

Drain in colander. Add to bowl with remaining ingredients and combine. Season with salt and pepper.

Stuffing for 12-to-16-pound turkey.

RAISIN STUFFING FOR CHICKEN

- 1 cup raisins
- 1¼ cup day old bread cubes
- ½ cup milk
  salt and pepper
  pinch of cinnamon

Scald raisins in water to cover them. Drain. Soak bread cubes in milk and squeeze excess out. Combine with raisins and season well with salt and pepper and pinch of cinnamon.

Stuffing for a 3-to-4-pound roasting chicken.

SHRIMP AND BACON STUFFING

- 8 slices bacon
- 8 tablespoons butter or ¼ pound
- ½ cup chopped shallots
- 3 cups day-old bread cubes
- ½ cup cooked shrimp, chopped
- ⅓ cup fresh chopped parsley
- 2 tablespoons white wine or dry vermounth
- 1 egg, lightly beaten
  salt and pepper to taste

Cook bacon until crisp. Drain and crumble. Melt 3 tablespoons butter and sauté shallots for 5 minutes. In large bowl combine crumbled bacon, sautéed shallots, 5 tablespoons melted butter and remaining ingredients. Season with salt and pepper.

Stuffing for 4-to-5½-pound roasting chicken or capon.

TURKEY PLAIN
AND FANCY

Benjamin Franklin wanted to name the turkey our national bird and somehow that would have been very fitting. Turkey, an American tradition at Thanksgiving, is also very popular for Christmas and other special occasions. However, turkey is available—and well worth the price—all year long, because, as the recipes that follow suggest, it offers a variety of totally different and inexpensive meals for families large and small.

In selecting a turkey, watch for fresh, firm birds with full breast and plump legs. It is best not to buy a turkey that is over 18 pounds because the larger turkeys tend to be drier and tougher. If you are having a crowd of guests, roast two medium-sized turkeys.

Frozen turkey is available the year round in markets and fresh turkey can be found in many butcher shops. Fresh turkey should be kept thoroughly chilled, and cooked within two days, for it is more perishable than chicken. The best method for thawing frozen turkey is to leave it in its wrapping in the refrigerator overnight, but directions are on the package. For quicker thawing, place the bird (in original wrapping) in cold water for 4 to 8 hours, depending on size. Change water occasionally. Do not use hot water.

To calculate the size of turkey needed, figure about one pound per person. A turkey can be roasted stuffed or unstuffed. If stuffing is used, it should be prepared and spooned into the bird just before roasting. Season the bird inside and out with salt and pepper. Loosely fill with stuffing. Sew opening closed, or use small skewers and lace closed. Stuff wishbone cavity and secure neck skin to back with a small skewer. Tie legs together and fold wings to back of turkey. The turkey can be fully trussed (see chicken) but it is not necessary.

ROAST TURKEY

Prepare bird as directed above. Preheat oven to 450°F. Remove giblets and prepare turkey stock for giblet gravy. Place bird in roasting pan in oven and immediately reduce heat to 325°F. Cook stuffed turkey about 25 minutes per pound: unstuffed, 18 to 20 minutes per pound. Baste often with butter throughout entire cooking or soak a cloth in butter and place over bird after 30 minutes of cooking. Baste with pan drippings occasionally and remove cloth the last 30 minutes of cooking so bird will brown nicely. Turkey is done when, after being pierced in thigh area, juice runs out clear. Drumsticks will also move easily up and down and flesh of drumstick will be soft to the touch. Roasting thermometer should register 180°F. to 185°F.

Remove trussing strings and skewers if used. Place turkey on heated platter and garnish with parsley or watercress. Allow bird to rest 20 to 30 minutes for easier carving. (See page 14.)

NOTE: Never partially roast bird and continue cooking later.

FOIL ROASTED TURKEY

The turkey takes less time to cook when it is roasted in foil and I find this method produces a slightly moister bird.

Lay a large sheet of wide heavy-duty foil across roasting pan. Place turkey—stuffed or unstuffed—on foil and brush well with butter. Season with salt and pepper. Cover wing tips with small folds of foil, then fold sheets of foil up around bird. It shouldn't be sealed airtight. If bird is very large two sheets of foil may be necessary. Place roasting pan in preheated 450°F. oven and roast according to chart below. Unstuffed turkey will require a little less cooking time.

WEIGHT	COOKING TIME
6 to 9 pounds	2 to 2½ hours
10 to 13 pounds	2¾ to 3 hours
14 to 18 pounds	3 to 3¼ hours
19 to 23 pounds	3½ to 3¾ hours

Fold the foil back during the last 30 minutes of cooking so that the turkey can brown nicely.

For carving see page 14.

BARBECUED TURKEY

1 6-to-8-pound young turkey
1 cup vinegar
¾ cup oil
1 cup tomato juice
3 tablespoons Worcestershire sauce
1 medium onion, minced
2 cloves garlic, crushed
1 teaspoon paprika
salt and pepper to taste

Combine vinegar, oil, tomato juice, Worcestershire sauce, onion, garlic, paprika, salt and pepper to taste. Truss turkey and baste with sauce. Roast according to roasting directions, basting frequently with sauce.

Serves 6 to 8.

BROILED TURKEY

1 7-to-8-pound young turkey
1 stick butter or ¼ pound
½ cup apple juice
1 tablespoon curry powder
½ teaspoon onion powder
¼ teaspoon garlic powder

Cut turkey in ½ and season with salt and pepper. Blend melted butter, apple juice, curry powder, onion powder, and garlic powder. Baste turkey with sauce and broil over coals for 50 to 60 minutes or until tender.

Serves 6.

CURRIED TURKEY EN BRIOCHE

2 cups cubed cooked turkey
3 tablespoons butter
1 medium onion, finely chopped
2 tablespoons flour
1¼ cups beef broth
½ cup orange juice
1 tablespoon sherry
¼ cup raisins
3 tablespoons chutney
⅛ teaspoon ground ginger
1 tablespoon curry powder
½ teaspoon grated orange peel
4 oversized brioche

In saucepan melt 3 tablespoons butter and cook onions for 5 minutes. Stir in flour and cook gently for 2 or 3 minutes. Slowly pour in combined beef broth, orange juice, and sherry and cook until sauce thickens. Add turkey, raisins, chutney, ginger, curry powder, and orange peel. Reduce heat to a simmer and cook for 5 minutes. Remove ball from top of brioche and set aside. Carefully scoop out interior of each brioche and fill with turkey-curry mixture. Replace brioche ball. Serve with shredded lettuce or tossed green salad.

Serves 4.

HARLEQUIN TURKEY SALAD

   3 cups cubed cooked turkey breast
24 cherry tomatoes, cut in half
24 large black olives, pitted and cut in half
  ½ cup olive oil
   3 tablespoons lemon juice
  ¼ teaspoon garlic powder
  ½ teaspoon onion powder
  ⅛ teaspoon powdered mustard
  ¼ teaspoon salt
    freshly ground pepper

Place turkey, halved tomatoes, and black olives in salad bowl. In separate bowl combine remaining ingredients and pour over turkey mixture. Gently toss. Pile on bed of crisp lettuce leaves.

Serves 4.

MOLE DE GUAJOLOTE

Mole de Guajolote *is a national dish of Mexico. According to legend, it was concocted in the seventeenth century by the nuns of Puebla for a visiting church dignitary.*

   1 12-pound turkey, disjointed
    salt
    flour
  ½ cup oil

Season turkey pieces with salt and dredge in flour. Brown turkey in heated oil on all sides. Transfer turkey to large pot and cover with water. Add 1 teaspoon salt and bring to a boil. Reduce heat and simmer for about 1½ hours or until tender. Remove turkey from pot and cool. Remove meat from bones and cut into serving pieces. Put bones and turkey carcass back into stock and add giblets. Simmer until ready to use in Mole Sauce. 4 cups or more will be required.

MOLE SAUCE

- 4 tablespoons butter
- 2 large onions, chopped
- 3 or 4 garlic cloves, chopped
- 1 large green pepper, chopped
- ¼ cup raisins
- 1 teaspoon cumin
- ½ teaspoon aniseed
- ¼ teaspoon coriander
- ¼ teaspoon cinnamon
- ½ cup peanut butter
- 3 tablespoons toasted sesame seeds
- 1 8-ounce can tomato sauce
- 2 medium tomatoes, peeled, seeded, and chopped
- 1 4-ounce can red chili peppers—or ¼ cup chili powder
- 4 toasted tortillas, broken (canned)
- ½ teaspoon salt
- 2 squares (2 ounces) bitter chocolate, grated
- 4 cups turkey stock

In large skillet melt butter and cook onions until they begin to color. Add garlic and green pepper. Cook until soft and put into blender with remaining ingredients using 2 cups of stock for liquid. When smooth, add remaining stock. Strain and correct seasoning with chili powder and salt. Add more stock if necessary. Pour into large saucepan and add turkey. Simmer for 15 to 25 minutes until sauce thickens, stirring often. Serve with rice.

Serves 8.

SPICY TURKEY

    1 8-pound turkey
    2 tablespoons flour
    1 teaspoon salt
    1 teaspoon pepper
    ½ teaspoon ground ginger
    1 teaspoon cinnamon
    1 teaspoon sugar
    1 large clove garlic, crushed
    2 large onions, quartered
    4 tablespoons soft butter

Mix flour, salt, pepper, ground ginger, cinnamon, sugar, and garlic. Rub turkey inside and out with this mixture, wrap in foil and refrigerate for 6 hours. Place bird in large pot and add onions and enough water to cover. Bring to a boil, reduce heat and simmer for 2 hours or until tender, but not falling apart. Drain and place in roasting pan. Spread butter over bird and bake in 425°F. oven until nicely browned. Baste occasionally with butter. Serve with roast potatoes, fresh green beans, and tomatoes cooked in olive oil.

Serves 6 to 8.

TURKEY AMANDINE

- 3 cups cubed cooked turkey
- 3 tablespoons butter
- ½ pound mushrooms, sliced
- 2 tablespoons flour
- 2 cups chicken broth
- ½ teaspoon salt
  pepper
- ¼ cup sherry
- 1 tablespoon soy sauce
- ½ cup toasted slivered almonds

Melt butter in Dutch oven or ovenproof casserole. Add mushrooms and cook for 5 minutes. Sprinkle flour over mushrooms and stir. Gradually pour in broth, stirring constantly. Season lightly with salt and pepper. Add sherry, soy sauce, turkey, and almonds. Bring to a boil, reduce heat, and simmer for 10 minutes. If sauce is too thick, add more chicken broth. Serve on rice.

Serves 4.

TURKEY BURGERS

    3 cups cooked turkey, minced or ground
1½ cups bread crumbs
    2 tablespoons sesame seeds
  ⅓ cup minced scallions
    1 teaspoon soy sauce
  ½ teaspoon prepared mustard
    2 eggs, beaten
      salt and pepper to taste
      butter

Combine turkey, bread crumbs, sesame seeds, and scallions. Add soy sauce, mustard, and eggs. Season to taste with salt and pepper. Shape into 8 patties and sauté in melted butter until golden on both sides. Serve on toasted buns; accompany with sliced tomato and Russian dressing.

Serves 4 to 6.

TURKEY DIVAN

    8 slices cooked turkey meat (or enough for
       4 servings)
    2 packages frozen broccoli spears
  ¾ cup hollandaise sauce
  ¾ cup Béchamel sauce
    2 tablespoons sherry
  ½ cup grated Parmesan cheese

Prepare broccoli according to package directions and arrange spears attractively on ovenproof serving platter. Top broccoli with slices of turkey. Blend hollandaise sauce with Béchamel sauce and sherry. Pour over chicken. Sprinkle Parmesan cheese liberally over sauce and place in hot oven under broiler until cheese is golden.

Serves 4.

TURKEY FILLETS PIEMONTESE
(*Filetti de tacchine alla Piemontese*)

8 slices raw turkey breast—about ⅓ inch
    thick and about 3 inches by 5 inches, have
    butcher prepare them
  salt and pepper
  flour for dredging
5 tablespoons butter, or as needed
½ cup Marsala wine
¾ cup chicken broth
4 truffles, thinly sliced (optional)
⅔ cup grated fresh Parmesan cheese

Sprinkle turkey fillets with salt and pepper and dredge each in flour on both sides. Shake off excess flour. Melt 2 tablespoons butter in large skillet and brown turkey fillets a few at a time on both sides. Add butter as needed. Transfer browned fillets to buttered baking dish. Cover and keep warm. Pour Marsala into skillet in which turkey browned. Bring to a boil, scraping up any particles on the bottom of the pan. Reduce wine to half, add chicken broth and 2 tablespoons butter. Bring to a boil. Meanwhile, cover browned turkey fillets with sliced truffles and grated

Parmesan cheese. Pour Marsala sauce into baking dish
with turkey and place in hot 450°F. oven until cheese
melts and turns golden.

Serves 4.

TURKEY FLORENTINE

> 8 slices cooked turkey or enough for 4 servings
> 2 packages frozen chopped spinach
> 2 teaspoons lemon juice
> 4 tablespoons butter
> 2 tablespoons flour
> ⅔ cup milk, heated
> ½ cup heavy cream, heated
> ½ cup grated Cheddar cheese
>   salt and pepper to taste
> ¼ cup dried bread crumbs

Cook spinach with lemon juice according to package
directions. Keep warm and set aside. In saucepan
melt 2 tablespoons butter, add flour, and slowly whisk
in heated combined milk and heavy cream. Cook,
stirring for 3 minutes and add cheese. Stir until cheese
melts and sauce is smooth and thickened. Season well
with salt and white pepper. In ovenproof serving dish
arrange drained spinach and top with turkey slices.
Spoon sauce over turkey and sprinkle with bread
crumbs. Dot with 2 tablespoons remaining butter.
Place in preheated oven under broiler until sauce and
bread crumbs are golden. Turn off broiler and leave
in oven for 1 minute. Serve immediately.

Serves 4.

TURKEY HASH

      3 cups cooked turkey, cut into small cubes
      3 tablespoons butter or as needed
      1 medium onion, finely chopped
      2 tablespoons green pepper, chopped
      4 or 5 large fresh mushrooms, diced
   1½ cups cooked potatoes, cut into small cubes
      ¼ cup chicken stock or as needed
        salt and pepper
        fresh chopped parsley

Melt butter in large skillet and sauté onions, green pepper, and mushrooms for 3 or 4 minutes. Add turkey, potatoes, and chicken stock then stir gently. Season and pat hash flat on top with spatula. Sauté over medium low heat until golden on bottom. Quickly, turn hash over on a flat lid or cookie sheet and slide back into pan. Add butter as needed and cook until crisp on underside. Serve on large heated platter garnished with parsley or place 4 poached eggs on top of hash.

Serves 4.

TURKEY LOAF

3 cups finely chopped cooked turkey
1 cup day-old bread crumbs
2 tablespoons butter
¾ cup milk, heated
2 eggs, beaten
2 stalks celery, minced
2 tablespoons pimiento, finely chopped
½ small green pepper, minced
1 medium onion, chopped fine
½ teaspoon salt
  pepper
1 cup white sauce
2 hard-boiled eggs

Combine all ingredients except white sauce and hard-boiled eggs. Mix thoroughly. Grease loaf pan and put in turkey mixture. Bake in preheated 350°F. oven for 30 to 35 minutes. Remove from oven and let stand at least 5 minutes before removing from pan. Turn out of pan upside down. Pour white sauce over loaf and garnish with slices of hard-boiled eggs.

Serves 6.

TURKEY MEXICANA

1 6-to-8-pound young turkey
  salt and pepper
4 tablespoons olive oil
2 cloves garlic, crushed
2 green peppers, coarsely chopped
2 firm ripe tomatoes, peeled and chopped

Cut turkey into serving pieces and season with salt and pepper. Heat olive oil in skillet and brown turkey on all sides. Transfer to side dish. Add garlic and green peppers to skillet. Sauté for about 5 minutes. Return turkey to pan, cover, and simmer for 1 hour, turning turkey occasionally. Add tomatoes and cook for 15 minutes longer or until turkey is tender.

Serves 6.

TURKEY SALAD ORIENTALE

3 to 4 cups cubed cooked turkey
1 3½-ounce can water chestnuts, chopped
½ cup toasted almond slivers
1 8-ounce can crushed pineapple
1 cup celery, chopped fine
1 cup seedless white grapes

DRESSING

1 cup mayonnaise
2 tablespoons curry powder
1 tablespoon lemon juice
1 tablespoon soy sauce

First place salad ingredients in large bowl and gently toss. In separate bowl blend together mayonnaise, curry powder, lemon juice, and soy sauce. Combine with turkey mixture and refrigerate at least 1 hour. Serve on lettuce leaves with sliced apples and bananas.

Serves 6.

TURKEY TETRAZZINI

Chicken Tetrazzini was named after the Italian opera singer Louisa Tetrazzini. I prefer the recipe made with turkey. It is a superb luncheon dish for a reception or social occasion. It also makes a nice surprise for the family the day after a roast turkey dinner. Green or plain noodles can replace the spaghetti.

2 cups diced cooked turkey
8 ounces spaghetti
salt
½ pound mushrooms, sliced
3 tablespoons butter
2 tablespoons flour
1 cup chicken or turkey stock
1 cup heavy cream
3 tablespoons sherry
salt and pepper
grated Parmesan cheese

Cook spaghetti in boiling water according to package directions. Drain and add a little butter to keep spaghetti from sticking together. Meanwhile, sauté sliced mushrooms in 3 tablespoons butter for 5 minutes. Sprinkle flour over mushrooms and stir. Add stock and cream, stirring constantly. Add sherry and turkey. Season. Butter a shallow baking dish and transfer spaghetti to dish. Pour turkey mixture over spaghetti and sprinkle liberally with grated Parmesan cheese. Bake in 400°F. oven for 25 minutes until golden.

Serves 4 to 6.

VENETIAN TURKEY

8 slices cooked breast of turkey, uniformly cut
3 tablespoons butter
1 medium onion, chopped
¼ pound fresh mushrooms, sliced
2 teaspoons paprika
½ teaspoon salt
  white pepper to taste
8 slices ham
¾ cup heavy cream
  fresh grated Parmesan cheese

Melt butter in skillet and cook onion for 5 minutes. Add mushrooms and cook 5 minutes more. Sprinkle paprika, salt and white pepper over mixture and stir. Transfer mushroom mixture to greased baking dish. Arrange turkey slices over mushrooms and top each slice with piece of ham. Pour cream over ham and sprinkle generously with Parmesan cheese. Bake in preheated 375°F. oven for about 25 minutes or until top turns golden.

Serves 4 to 6.

OTHER DOMESTIC BIRDS

CAPON

The flesh of a capon (a desexed male chicken) is particularly tender and delicate in flavor. Capon can be cooked in the same manner as other chicken or turkey. Capons weigh between 6 and 8 pounds and have a larger proportion of white meat. If you are serving 8 to 16 people, roast two capons.

CAPON À L'ANGLAISE

1 6-pound capon
2 quarts water
1 large onion, chopped
1 bay leaf
3 or 4 sprigs parsley
2 stalks celery, quartered
1 tablespoon salt
1 cup rich Béchamel sauce
¼ cup diced cooked tongue
2 packages frozen cauliflower
2 packages frozen baby carrots

Truss capon and place in deep pot. Add water, onion, bay leaf, parsley, celery, and salt. Bring to a boil, reduce heat to a simmer and cook covered until tender, about 1½ hours. Transfer capon to heated serving platter and remove trussing string. Cover capon with Béchamel sauce and sprinkle with diced cooked tongue. Surround with cauliflower heads and baby carrots cooked according to package directions.

Serves 4 to 6.

CAPON À LA MATIGNON

1 5-or-6-pound capon
  salt and pepper
4 tablespoons butter
3 carrots, sliced
3 stalks celery, sliced
3 medium onions, chopped
1 tablespoon fresh chopped parsley
½ cup rich chicken or veal stock
½ cup Madeira
¼ teaspoon thyme

Season cavity of capon with salt and pepper, then truss bird. Melt 4 tablespoons butter in heavy skillet and cook carrots, celery, and onions for 5 minutes. Add parsley, thyme, and season with salt and pepper. Transfer to heavy deep casserole large enough to hold capon. Place capon on bed of vegetables and pour remaining melted butter over capon. Cover and place in preheated 350°F. oven for about 1 hour and 40 minutes or until bird is done. Baste often with juice and butter in pot. Remove lid during last ½ hour of cooking. Pour stock and Madeira over capon and baste. Transfer capon to heated serving dish. Strain juices in pot and serve as sauce with capon. Thicken sauce with a little flour if desired.

Serves 4 to 6.

CAPON BRAISED IN CHAMPAGNE

1 6-pound capon
   salt and pepper
5 tablespoons butter, or as needed
1 carrot, minced
1 medium onion, chopped
4 mushrooms, chopped
2 cups champagne
¾ cup heavy cream

Salt and pepper cavity of capon. Truss. In bottom of large ovenproof casserole melt 3 tablespoons butter and gently brown capon on all sides. Remove capon and add carrot, onion, and mushrooms and a little more butter if needed. Cook over medium high heat for 3 or 4 minutes, stirring often. Replace capon in casserole and pour 1½ cups champagne over capon, cover and place in preheated 350°F. oven for about 1½ to 2 hours. Remove cover the last 20 minutes of cooking. Test by piercing thickest part of lower thigh. If juice comes out clear or pale yellow, bird is done.

Transfer capon to side dish and keep warm. Put casserole on burner on top of stove and add ½ cup remaining champagne and boil for 4 to 5 minutes. Strain and pour into clean saucepan. Add cream and heat thoroughly. Swirl in 2 tablespoons butter. Adjust seasoning. Pour a little sauce over capon and serve remainder in sauceboat. Surround capon with parslied potatoes and cooked, fresh whole string beans.

Serves 6.

SAVORY ROAST CAPON WITH SWEET POTATO STUFFING

    1 6-to-8-pound capon
       salt
    2 cups boiled chestnuts, diced
    6 tablespoons butter
    1 medium onion, chopped
    1 stalk celery, minced
    2 pounds sweet potatoes, boiled and mashed
    ¼ teaspoon thyme
       pepper

Season cavity of capon with salt. Mash 1 cup chestnuts and chop other cup. Melt 2 tablespoons butter in skillet and cook onion and celery for 5 minutes. In large bowl put mashed and chopped chestnuts, mashed sweet potatoes, 4 tablespoons melted butter, onion and celery mixture, and thyme. Season with salt and pepper. Fill body cavity of capon with stuffing, sew opening shut and tie legs together. Roast in preheated 350°F. oven about 20 minutes per pound or until tender, basting occasionally with pan drippings.

Serves 6 to 8.

CAPON SAVARIN

1 6-to-8-pound capon
   salt and pepper
   butter for basting
½ pound sausage
3 cups corn bread, crumbled
12 boiled chestnuts, chopped
½ cup diced cooked sweet potatoes
6 tablespoons butter
2 stalks celery, minced
1 medium onion, chopped
¼ pound mushrooms, chopped
1 egg, beaten
½ teaspoon thyme
½ teaspoon sage

Wash and pat capon dry. Season cavity with salt and pepper. Set aside to prepare stuffing. Cook sausage and mash with fork, crumbling it until no pink color remains. Drain in colander. In large bowl put sausage, corn bread, chopped chestnuts, and diced sweet potatoes. Melt 3 tablespoons butter in skillet and sauté celery and onion for 5 minutes. Add 3 tablespoons remaining butter and mushrooms, and continue cooking slowly for 4 more minutes. Put the skillet ingredients along with pan juices in bowl and add beaten egg, thyme, and sage. Gently blend.

Fill bird's body cavity loosely with stuffing. Sew opening closed and tie legs together. Place breast side up in roasting pan and brush capon with melted butter. Put in preheated 425°F. oven and immediately reduce heat to 325°F. Cook about 20 to 25 minutes per pound or until done.

Serves 6 to 8.

CORNISH GAME HEN

Cornish game hens are the smallest member of the chicken family. The best weigh only about 1 pound, though some come slightly larger. They have a subtle sweet flavor and provide a succulent dish for company. Unless the hens are unusually large, allow 1 bird for each person.

Frozen Cornish game hens are available in large markets. Thaw before cooking. The hens can be roasted whole, cut in half and fried, broiled, or baked. Few cookbooks offer enough recipes for these unusually flavorful birds, so I've tried to include several interesting ones here.

BIRDS OF PARADISE

4 Cornish game hens
  salt and pepper
3 tablespoons butter
1 medium onion, chopped
½ cup chicken broth
1 cup white wine
1 bay leaf
1 tablespoon fresh chopped parsley
½ teaspoon dried basil

Season trussed birds with salt and pepper and brown on all sides in butter. Transfer to roasting pan. Sauté onion for 5 minutes in pan where birds were browned. Add chicken broth, white wine, bay leaf, parsley, and basil. Bring to a boil and pour into roasting pan, cover, and cook in preheated 350°F. oven for approximately 50 minutes. Remove cover and cook 10 minutes longer. Meanwhile, prepare Saffron Rice recipe below. Place birds on bed of saffron rice and surround with alternating grilled tomatoes, pineapple slices, and sautéed green pepper strips.

SAFFRON RICE

- 2 cups long-grained rice
- 4 cups chicken stock
- ¾ cup water
- ½ teaspoon powdered saffron
- ½ cup chopped onions
- 2 tablespoons butter
- 2 teaspoons salt

Bring chicken stock and water to a boil. Add remaining ingredients. Stir and bring to a boil again. Reduce heat to simmer, cover, and cook until rice is tender, about 25 minutes.

Serves 4.

CORNISH GAME HENS STUFFED WITH WILD RICE MIXTURE

- 4 Cornish game hens
- 1 package wild rice mixture
- 3 tablespoons butter
- 1 medium onion, chopped fine
- 6 fresh mushrooms, chopped
- ½ teaspoon grated orange rind
  salt and pepper to taste
- ½ cup dry white wine

Cook wild rice mixture according to package directions. Set aside. In skillet melt butter and sauté onion for 5 minutes. Add mushrooms and cook 4 minutes longer. Add onion and mushrooms and any leftover butter to rice mixture along with orange rind. Combine gently. Season if necessary. Rub Cornish hens with salt and pepper and stuff with rice. Sew up openings. Place in large baking pan and add ½ cup white wine. Cover with lid or tinfoil and bake in preheated 400°F. oven for 30 minutes. Remove cover and cook 15 minutes more.

Serves 4.

CORNSH GAME HENS
WITH RICH MUSHROOM SAUCE

4 Cornish game hens
3 slices bacon, chopped
3 tablespoons butter
4 shallots, minced
½ pound mushrooms, minced
¼ teaspoon thyme
1 tablespoon fresh chopped parsley
  salt and pepper to taste
½ cup chicken stock
½ cup dry white wine
1 tablespoon lemon juice
4 slices fried day-old bread, crust trimmed off

In large casserole fry bacon until crisp. Remove bacon with slotted spoon and drain on absorbent paper and set aside. Truss birds and brown all over in bacon drippings. Transfer birds to side dish. Add 3 tablespoons butter, shallots, mushrooms, thyme, and parsley to drippings left in pan. Season with salt and pepper. Cook 5 to 8 minutes. Add stock, wine, and lemon juice. Place Cornish game hens in mushroom mixture, cover, and put in preheated 350°F. oven for 40 to 45 minutes. Serve each bird on slice of fried bread and spoon mushroom sauce over it. Garnish with crisp bacon.

Serves 4.

GRILLED CORNISH GAME HENS
WITH BACON

4 small Cornish game hens
   salt and pepper
4 tablespoons butter, melted
1 tablespoon lemon juice
8 slices bacon, partially cooked

Butterfly each game hen by cutting through backbone enough to flatten slightly. Season birds with salt and pepper. Baste with melted butter and lemon juice mixed. Place birds skin side down on broiler rack. Broil for 5 minutes. Turn birds again, baste, and cook 5 to 7 minutes. Finally, turn hens breast side up. Place 2 pieces of partially cooked bacon across each bird. Broil until bacon is crisp and bird is golden and tender. Serve on large heated platter garnished with half a bunch of watercress at each end.

Serves 4.

PINEAPPLE-GLAZED CORNISH
GAME HENS

4 Cornish game hens
   salt and pepper
¼ cup melted butter
¼ cup canned frozen concentrated pineapple
   juice
2 tablespoons vinegar
3 tablespoons brown sugar

Truss birds and season with salt and pepper. Brush with butter and place in reheated 350°F. oven for 30 minutes, basting with butter occasionally. Meanwhile, prepare pineapple glaze by blending concentrated pineapple juice, vinegar, and brown sugar. Brush on birds and continue roasting for 30 minutes more, basting often with pineapple glaze.

Serves 4.

DUCK

Roast duck is a delicious treat and my favorite way of preparing duck, but it can also be braised or fricasseed with excellent results. Ducks are available, frozen, in markets throughout the country. Fresh, ice-chilled ducks can also be found in butcher shops and some markets. The fresh ducks should be kept thoroughly chilled—wrapped in foil or wax paper—and used within two days. Frozen duck should be left in its original wrapping to thaw in the refrigerator for 1 to 1½ days and then used immediately.

Several important things should be done before the duck is ready to roast. Because there is a layer of fat under the duck's skin, it is best to prick the skin in several places with a skewer or sharp two-tined carving fork. This allows the fat to escape easily during cooking. The fat should be siphoned or spooned away as it is expelled during cooking. Also pull out or cut away extra fat around the inside of vent opening before roasting. No basting is required unless you want a special coating. Be sure to remove giblets and use to make duck stock for giblet gravy.

Duck can be served stuffed or unstuffed. After stuffing lightly sew opening closed and tie legs loosely together. Allow 15 to 20 minutes of cooking per pound unstuffed; 20 to 25 minutes per pound stuffed. No matter what other recipes claim a 3-to-4 pound duck will serve only two people. A 5-pound duck, quartered, will just serve four. Accordingly, duck should either be cut in half with poultry shears or quartered when served.

BASIC ROAST DUCK
AND SAUCE

1 4½-to-5-pound duck and liver
  salt and pepper
1 medium onion, peeled and left whole
1 large slice of cooking apple
3 medium onions, peeled and quartered
3 carrots, peeled and chopped
¼ cup red wine or port
2 tablespoons butter

DUCK STOCK

2 cups chicken broth
1 cup water
  neck and giblets from duck
¼ teaspoon thyme
1 stalk celery, chopped
1 medium onion, chopped

Season body cavity of duck with salt and pepper. Place whole onion, slice of apple, and duck liver inside and sew opening closed. Tie legs together. Prick skin around thickest part of thighs and dry duck with paper towels or towel. Place duck, breast side up, in roasting pan and surround with quartered onions and carrots. In preheated 450°F. oven, place pan on middle rack and roast for 15 minutes. Reduce heat to 350°F. and cook for 1 hour. Test for doneness by pricking lower thigh. When the juice that runs out is pale yellow or clear it is done. If tinges of pink remain duck is not fully cooked.

Once duck is in the oven prepare duck stock. Put

water and chicken broth in saucepan and add duck neck and giblets, 1 stalk celery, thyme, and onion. Bring to a boil, reduce heat to a simmer and cook for 1¼ hours. After 30 minutes of cooking, season with salt and pepper. When duck is done, remove trussing strings and discard onion, apple, and liver. Place duck on heated serving platter and keep warm. In roasting pan remove all but 1 tablespoon of duck fat and leave carrots and onion in pan. Pour in 2 cups strained duck stock. Bring to a boil. Scrape bottom of pan for any particles that remain and mash vegetables. Adjust seasoning. Pour in ¼ cup red wine or port and simmer a few minutes. Swirl in 2 tablespoons butter and melt in sauce, strain. Pour some of sauce over duck and serve remaining sauce in heated sauceboat.

Serves 4.

BRAISED DUCK WITH MUSHROOMS

      1 4½-to-5-pound duck
      7 tablespoons butter
   2½ cups water
      1 teaspoon salt
      ¼ teaspoon pepper
      1 medium onion, sliced
      3 sprigs parsley
         pinch rosemary or thyme
      ½ pound mushrooms, sliced
      2 tablespoons flour
      ½ cup red wine

In large heavy pot heat 4 tablespoons butter and brown duck on all sides. Pour off fat. Add water, salt, pepper, onion, parsley, and rosemary or thyme; bring to a boil, reduce heat, cover, and simmer for 1¼ hours. Meanwhile, sauté mushrooms in remaining 3 tablespoons butter for about 5 minutes. Sprinkle flour over mushrooms and stir. Drain stock from duck and strain. Pour strained stock into mushrooms, add red wine, stirring constantly until creamy and thickened. Pour back over duck, cover, and simmer another 10 minutes. Remove duck and carve into serving pieces. Pour sauce over it and serve.

Serves 4.

CANETON A L'ORANGE
(Duck with Orange Sauce)

Caneton à l'Orange, a magnificent classic French dish, is served in many restaurants in the United States. Its preparation takes time and care, but I think you will discover you'll like it even better when it comes from your own kitchen.

First prepare duck stock by placing duck's giblets and neck in saucepan with 4 chicken backs and bouquet garni made of: 1 bay leaf, 3 sprigs parsley, pinch of thyme, 4 peppercorns, 1 stalk celery—chopped, 1 teaspoon salt, and 1 medium chopped onion. Add 1 quart water and bring to a boil, reduce heat and simmer for 1½ to 2 hours until 2 cups of strained rich duck stock remain.

1 5-pound duck
1 3-inch by 1-inch strip of orange peel
6 navel oranges
1 lemon
¼ cup sugar
¼ cup wine vinegar
2 cups duck stock (see above)
4 tablespoons Curaçao or Cointreau
½ cup dry white wine
   salt and pepper to taste
2 tablespoons butter

Season duck cavity with salt and pepper. Place 3-inch strip of orange peel in duck and truss. Prick lower thighs and breast with fork so grease can be released easily. Put duck in preheated 350°F. oven for 1 hour and 30 minutes or until juices are clear when pricked in the thigh with fork. Remove fat from pan as it is expelled.

Peel the zest (outer layer of skin—no white) from 2 oranges and 1 lemon. Squeeze juice from these oranges and lemon and put in a bowl. Cut zest into fine julienne strips (1/16 inch wide by 1½ inches long) and drop them into 3 cups of boiling water and cook for 10 minutes. Drain and dry on paper towels. Peel 4 remaining oranges and cut into neat sections. Remove any skin. Cover in bowl and set aside.

To prepare sauce a caramel must first be made. Melt sugar in a saucepan over medium low heat and as it begins to turn golden pour in wine vinegar. When caramel in color, remove from heat and add orange and lemon juice. Pour in 1 cup duck stock then simmer for a few minutes and add remaining cup of duck stock. Mix cornstarch with Curaçao or Cointreau and stir into sauce. Simmer until sauce is clear and slightly thickened. Adjust seasoning, cover, and set aside.

When duck is done, remove trussing and orange peel. Transfer to heated platter and return to turned-off oven. Pour away fat from roasting pan, add wine, and place over high heat, scraping bottom of pan for coagulated particles. Reduce to ½ and strain through fine sieve into sauce and bring to a boil. Swirl in butter. Top duck with orange and lemon strips and surround duck with orange segments. Spoon a few tablespoons of sauce over duck. Serve rest of sauce in heated sauceboat.

Serves 4.

DUCK AND RED CABBAGE

1 5-pound duck
  salt
3 tablespoons butter
1 medium-large onion
1 medium red cabbage, shredded
1 tablespoon lemon juice
1 cup white wine
1 teaspoon sugar

Wash and pat duck dry. Season with salt inside and out. Roast in 350°F. oven for 1 hour. Melt butter in large skillet and cook onion for 5 minutes. Add cabbage and cook for 3 or 4 minutes. Add lemon juice, wine, and sugar and season with salt and pepper. Cover and simmer for 15 minutes. Remove duck from roasting pan and drain off all grease. Place cabbage in roasting pan and top with duck. Return to oven and cook for 45 minutes more or until tender.

Serves 4.

DUCK CASSOULET

1 5-pound roasted duck, meat removed from
    bones and cut into small serving pieces
1 pound dried white beans
1 teaspoon salt
¼ teaspoon pepper
2 large onions, chopped
2 cloves garlic, crushed
1 carrot, chopped
1 bay leaf
  pinch thyme
1 garlic sausage, cut into 1-inch lengths
4 tablespoons butter
2 teaspoons flour
1 cup dry white wine
2 tomatoes, peeled and chopped

Soak beans in water overnight. Next day drain beans and cover them with fresh water. Add salt, pepper, 1 chopped onion, garlic, carrot, bay leaf, and pinch of thyme. Bring to a boil, reduce heat and simmer 1½ hours. Meanwhile, brown duck and sausage in butter. Transfer to earthenware pot or casserole. Sauté remaining chopped onion in pan where duck was browned for 5 to 8 minutes until it begins to turn golden. Sprinkle flour over onions and stir. Add wine and tomatoes; bring to a boil and simmer for 5 minutes. Add to beans and continue cooking for ½ hour more.

Transfer beans to casserole with duck and sausage. Bake, uncovered, in preheated 350°F. oven for 35 to 45 minutes.

Serves 4.

A crisp green salad, crusty French bread, and a Bordeaux or Burgundy wine are perfect accompaniments to this typical French fare.

DUCK WITH CHERRIES

1 5-pound duck
salt and pepper
3 tablespoons cognac
½ cup dry white wine
¼ cup chicken stock
pinch cinnamon
1 tablespoon sugar or to taste
2 cups Bing cherries, pitted

Season cavity of duck with salt and pepper and tie legs loosely together. Place in preheated 350°F. oven for 1½ hours or until done. Pour cognac over duck and ignite. Cut duck in quarters and place on heated serving dish. In the roasting pan, bring wine, stock, cinnamon, and sugar to a boil; add cherries, cover and simmer about 5 minutes. Pour cherries and sauce over duck pieces.

Serves 4.

DUCK WITH LENTILS

1 4½-to-5-pound duck
4 strips bacon, cut into small pieces
1 clove garlic, crushed
1 medium onion, chopped fine
1 carrot, minced
1 stalk celery, minced
1 tablespoon flour
¼ teaspoon dried thyme
1 tablespoon fresh chopped parsley
¼ teaspoon freshly ground pepper
1 teaspoon salt
2 cups dried lentils
1 cup beef broth
3 cups water

Sauté bacon until half done. Add garlic, onion, carrot, celery, and cook for 5 minutes. Sprinkle flour over mixture and stir. Add thyme, parsley, pepper, salt, lentils, beef broth, and water. Bring to a boil, cover, and simmer for 1 hour and 45 minutes. Meanwhile, tie ducks legs loosely together and roast in preheated 375°F. oven for 1 hour and 15 minutes. Quarter duck and put in pot with lentils; cover and continue cooking ½ hour more or until lentils are tender. Add more water if necessary. Transfer duck to heated serving dish. Ladle a little of the lentils over duck and serve the remainder in another heated dish.

Serves 4.

EASY DUCK WITH ORANGE SAUCE

1 4-pound duck
 salt and pepper
4 tablespoons sugar
1 tablespoon wine vinegar
 juice of 2 oranges
 grated rind of 1 orange
⅓ cup Grand Marnier

Season duck inside and out with salt and pepper and roast in 375°F. oven for 1¼ hours or until done. Ten to 15 minutes before duck is done, prepare sauce. Bring sugar and vinegar to a boil until it carmelizes. Add orange juice, Grand Marnier, and grated rind, stirring constantly. Add 2 or 3 tablespoons of drippings from duck. Place duck in heated serving dish and pour sauce over duck.

Serves 3 to 4.

FRICASSEE OF DUCK

1 4½-pound duck
 salt and pepper
4 tablespoons butter
1 medium onion, chopped
1 bay leaf
1 stalk celery, chopped
3 cups chicken stock
½ cup chopped mushrooms

Cut duck into serving pieces. Season with salt and pepper. Brown duck in butter. Pour off fat. Add onion, bay leaf, celery, and stock. Bring to a boil, cover and simmer until tender, about 1 hour. Ten minutes before duck is done add mushrooms. Serve with buttered noodles.

Serves 4.

HONEY-COATED DUCK WITH APRICOT SAUCE

    1 4-pound duck
    2 tablespoons honey
    1 16-ounce can apricot halves
    2 tablespoons lemon juice
    ½ teaspoon grated lemon rind
    1 tablespoon cornstarch
    1 tablespoon sugar
    1 tablespoon butter
    ⅛ teaspoon garlic powder
    ⅛ teaspoon salt
    3 tablespoons apricot brandy

Roast duck in preheated 375°F. oven for 45 minutes. Brush duck with honey and return to oven for 30 minutes or until done. Meanwhile, prepare sauce. Use juice from can of apricot halves, add lemon juice, and enough water to make 1 cup of liquid. Put into saucepan and add grated lemon rind, cornstarch, sugar, butter, garlic powder, and salt. Whisk while bringing to a boil until smooth and thickened. Reduce heat and add chopped apricots and apricot brandy. Heat thoroughly, but don't boil. Place cooked duck on heated serving dish, pour a little sauce over duck and serve the remainder in a sauceboat. Garnish with fresh watercress.

Serves 2 to 3.

PAVILLY DUCK
(*Canard à la Pavilly*)

1 4-pound duck
  duck liver, minced
2 large tart cooking apples, peeled, cored, and sliced
6 shallots
⅛ teaspoon powdered sage
¼ teaspoon each salt and pepper
2 tablespoons butter
  juice of one orange
  petit pois (small green peas)

Combine minced liver, sliced apples, shallots, sage, salt, pepper, and butter. Stuff duck's body cavity, sew opening closed and tie legs together. Roast in very hot oven at 450° F. for about 40 minutes. Remove and take out stuffing. Carve breast and legs of duck into thin slices. Remove as much of juices from roasting pan as possible. Mix into stuffing. Pile the stuffing into a hot serving dish (ovenproof) and arrange the slices of duck on the stuffing. Sprinkle with orange juice and return to hot oven for 8 to 10 minutes. Serve dish with a border of petit pois.

Serves 2 to 3.

ROAST DUCK WITH
PINEAPPLE SAUSAGE STUFFING

        1 4½-to-5-pound duck
     2½ cups cooked rice
        ¾ pound country sausage, crumbled
        1 medium onion, chopped
        2 stalks celery, chopped
        2 tablespoons butter
        1 cup canned crushed pineapple and juice
        2 tablespoons raisins (optional)
            salt and pepper

Wash duck and pat dry. Cook rice. To prepare
stuffing, cook sausage with onion and celery until
sausage is no longer pink. Drain in colander. Return
to skillet. Add butter, cooked rice, pineapple, raisins,
if used, and season with salt and pepper. Fill duck cavity with stuffing and sew up vent and tie legs loosely
together. Prick lower thighs so grease will be easily
released. Roast in 375°F. oven for 2 hours. Serve
with the orange sauce.

ORANGE SAUCE

        1 cup orange juice
       ½ cup giblet broth or chicken broth
       ½ teaspoon grated orange rind
       ½ cup sugar
        1 tablespoon cornstarch
            large pinch nutmeg

Mix all ingredients in saucepan and heat until sugar
dissolves and sauce thickens.

Serves 4.

ROAST DUCK WITH
SAUSAGE AND APPLE STUFFING

1 4½-to-5-pound duck
½ pound pork sausage
4 tart cooking apples, peeled, cored, and sliced
2 tablespoons sugar
¼ teaspoon sage
¼ teaspoon cinnamon
  salt and pepper to taste
2 tablespoons brandy
¼ cup red wine
¼ cup beef broth

Trim fat from cavity of duck and rub inside with salt and pepper. In skillet sauté sausage until slightly browned, crumbling it apart with a fork. Put in colander to drain. Meanwhile, add apples to skillet and sauté for 4 or 5 minutes. Drain. Mix sausage, apple slices, sugar, sage, cinnamon, salt and pepper, and brandy together. Bring wine and broth to a boil and cook for 4 or 5 minutes. Pour into sausage mixture. Gently blend and stuff duck. Sew opening closed and tie legs together. Place in roasting pan and roast in preheated 350°F. oven allowing 25 minutes per pound. Approximately 2 hours if 5-pound duck is used.

Serves 4.

SALMIS OF DUCK
(*Canard en Salmi*)

1 4-pound duck and liver
1 large onion, finely chopped
3 tablespoons butter
¼ pound mushrooms, diced
⅔ cup duck stock
3 tablespoons red burgundy
2 tablespoons brandy
  salt and pepper
  butter-fried croutons

Put liver inside untrussed bird and cook about 30 minutes in very hot 450°F. oven. Reduce heat to 350°F. and cook 30 minutes more. Remove from oven. Transfer liver to side dish and save. Carve breast and legs into thin slices and put into well-buttered ovenproof dish and set aside. Meanwhile, sauté the onion in butter until golden and add mushrooms for the last 5 minutes of cooking. Now add finely chopped liver, stock, and wine. Season with salt and pepper. Sprinkle duck with brandy and pour onion mushroom mixture over the slices of duck and put back in hot oven for about 10 minutes. Serve surrounded with fried croutons.

Serves 2.

SOY-GLAZED ROAST DUCK

- 1 5-pound duck
- 3 tablespoons sherry
- ½ cup honey
- ½ cup soy sauce
- 2 teaspoons Worcestershire sauce
- 1 teaspoon fresh grated ginger
  pinch nutmeg
- 2 cloves garlic, crushed

Dry duck and let stand for ½ hour. Tie legs together. Place in preheated 350°F. oven. Mix together remaining ingredients and baste duck often for 1½ hours or until duck is done. Duck will have a rich mahogany-glazed color.

Serves 4.

SPICY BRAISED DUCK

- 1 4½-to-5-pound duck, quartered
- 1 cup water
- 1 large carrot, quartered
- 1 stalk celery, quartered
- ½ teaspoon salt
  pepper to taste
- 2 tablespoons butter
- 1 medium onion, finely chopped
- 1 pimiento, chopped
- 2 tablespoons peanut butter
- 2 tablespoons flour
  dash cayenne pepper
  fresh chopped parsley

Place duck in large skillet and pour in water. Add carrot, celery, and salt and pepper. Bring to a boil, reduce heat, and simmer covered for 1½ hours. In separate skillet melt butter and sauté onion until transparent. Transfer cooked duck to side dish. Discard carrots, celery, and as much grease released from duck as possible from sauce. Strain sauce and put in clean saucepan. Add cooked onion, pimiento, peanut butter, flour, and cayenne pepper. Whisk until smooth and slightly thickened. Adjust seasoning. Spoon sauce over duck quarters and garnish with fresh chopped parsley.

Serves 4.

GOOSE

Goose, a Christmas tradition in European countries, is becoming more popular in this country. It can now be found in larger markets frozen and ready to cook. Goose provides a rich and delicious meal, so the next time you're choosing the main course for an important dinner, try goose.

An 8-pound goose is perfect for cooking, but anything under 12 pounds is fine. Goose may be cooked stuffed or unstuffed. Allow ½ cup to ¾ cup stuffing per pound of bird. Remove fat from inside goose around vent opening. This fat can be kept, rendered and used for cooking (see directions below). After stuffing bird, sew opening closed or lace closed with skewers and tie legs loosely together. Goose legs are very short and make it impossible to truss a goose as one would a turkey or chicken. Rub goose with lemon and salt. Prick goose in several places around thighs and lower breast areas so that the excess fat is released easily. Spoon or siphon off this fat as it accumulates. A cup of hot water in the roasting pan will keep the fat that is released from burning. Add more water if necessary. Roast the goose 20 to 25 minutes per pound if stuffed, a little less if unstuffed. Test for doneness by moving legs; if they move up and down easily the goose is done. Or pierce the thickest part of its thigh and if juice runs out clear goose is done.

Side dishes that go particularly well with goose are red cabbage, Brussels sprouts, sauerkraut, apples, or prunes. Goose stuffed with chestnuts is excellent—see the chestnut recipe under *Stuffing* heading.

Prepare gravy the same as other giblet gravy, pouring off most of fat.

Goose Fat

Pull or cut the goose fat from inside vent opening. Chop pieces and put into pan and cover with water, bring to a boil, cover and simmer until fat dissolves and water evaporates. Spattering sound will stop when only fat remains. Strain and place in jar, cool, and refrigerate until used. This goose fat can be used to cook or season potatoes, sauerkraut, and cabbage. Melted it can also be spread on crusty bread and seasoned with salt and pepper. This may be an acquired taste, but one worth cultivating.

CHRISTMAS ROAST GOOSE
WITH PRUNES AND APPLES
(Danish Style)

    1 8-to-10-pound goose
    1 lemon, cut in half
      salt and pepper
    2 cups chopped dried prunes
    2 cups sliced tart cooking apples, peeled,
        cored, and sliced
 1½ cups chicken stock
    2 tablespoons flour
    2 tablespoons butter
    1 tablespoon red currant jelly, or to taste

Rub inside cavity of goose with lemon and season with salt and pepper. Mix together prunes and apples.

Stuff bird with fruit mixture, sew up opening and tie legs together. Rub goose all over with lemon and sprinkle with salt and pepper. Pour chicken stock in roasting pan then place goose in pan. Roast in pre-heated 325°F. oven for about 25 minutes per pound or until legs move easily. Baste goose often with liquid in pan. Make goose giblet stock with giblets while cooking goose. When goose is done transfer to heated serving platter and wait about ½ hour before carving. Meanwhile, remove all but 3 tablespoons of fat from roasting pan. Add 2 cups strained giblet stock. Bring to a boil. Blend flour with butter and add to boiling gravy. Cook for about 5 minutes. Add red currant jelly, season well with salt and pepper. Strain and serve with goose.

Serves 8.

STUFFED GOOSE WITH ONIONS AND SAGE

- 1 8-to-10-pound goose
- 6 tablespoons butter
- 3 large onions
- 1 cup bread crumbs
- 2 tablespoons dried sage
- 2 teaspoons brown sugar
- 1 teaspoon prepared mustard
- 1 teaspoon salt
  pepper to taste

Melt butter and cook onions until transparent. Remove from heat. Combine with bread crumbs, sage, brown sugar, mustard, salt and pepper. Stuff goose;

sew opening closed and tie legs together. Place in preheated 400°F. oven and cook 30 minutes. Reduce heat
to 350°F. and continue cooking about 2 hours longer
or until done, depending on size of goose.

Serves 6 to 8.

GOOSE WITH APPLE
AND RAISIN STUFFING

    1 8-to-10-pound goose
    1 lemon, cut in half
    3 cups sliced cooking apples
    1 cup finely chopped onion
    1 cup raisins
    6 to 7 cups bread cubes
    1 teaspoon salt
    ¼ teaspoon pepper
    2 tablespoons sugar
    ¾ cup butter

Rub goose with lemon and season inside and out
with salt and pepper. Remove fat from inside goose
around vent opening. Combine remaining ingredients
and stuff goose, sew opening closed. Place in roasting
pan with 1 cup water. Roast in preheated 325°F. oven
for approximately 25 minutes per pound.

Serves 6.

GOOSE WITH
SAUERKRAUT STUFFING

1 8-to-10-pound goose
  salt and pepper
2 tablespoons goose fat
1 large onion, chopped
2 pounds sauerkraut
1 teaspoon caraway seeds
1 teaspoon paprika
1½ cups toasted croutons
¼ cup white wine

Trim off fat from inside goose. Wipe goose dry and rub with salt and pepper inside. In small skillet add several pieces of goose fat and cook until rendered to liquid fat. When there is 2 tablespoons of fat, discard remaining solid pieces. Add onion and sauté until golden. Put sauerkraut in colander and rinse with water. When thoroughly drained, place in large bowl. Add onion, caraway seeds, paprika, croutons, and white wine. Stuff goose with sauerkraut mixture, sew opening closed, and tie legs together. Roast in preheated 350°F. oven approximately 25 minutes per pound. Serve with gravy made from drippings in roasting pan and giblet stock.

Serves 6 to 8.

GOOSE AND ORANGE SALAD

2 cups cubed cooked goose
2 cups orange slices
1 cup chopped celery
1 medium red onion, chopped
½ cup vegetable oil
3 tablespoons wine vinegar
¼ teaspoon dried mustard
¼ teaspoon onion powder
¼ teaspoon salt or to taste
    pepper to taste
½ cup toasted almond slivers

Place goose, orange slices, celery, and onion in large bowl. In separate bowl mix oil, vinegar, dried mustard, onion powder, salt and pepper. Pour over goose mixture and gently toss. Let set 10 minutes. Place on lettuce leaves and garnish with toasted almond slivers.

Serves 4 to 6.

PRESERVED GOOSE or CONFIT D'OIE

1 8-to-12-pound goose
    salt
    cold water

Quarter goose and cut away all fat from the inside. Rub goose well all over with salt. Melt goose fat with ½ cup cold water in heavy casserole and add goose pieces. Cover and simmer for 2½ hours. Remove casserole and let stand until fat settles. Sprinkle salt generously inside deep crock or pot and place 1 inch of the goose fat in the bottom. Add goose and cover with remaining fat. (Don't use any of the goose juices.) Cover tightly and keep in cool place for 4 or 5 months. When ready to use goose, remove fat from around goose. Superb in a cassoulet or with lentils or other beans. Very good simply sautéed.

PIGEON

Pigeons are generally available all year long. They are meaty little birds and are best braised, stewed, or in a casserole, ragout, or pie. They can be roasted if they aren't too old (older ones tend to be tough) by placing a piece of butter in the cavity of the bird and wrapping a piece of lard or bacon over the breast. Depending on size, allow a half or whole bird for each person.

BRAISED STUFFED PIGEONS

4 pigeons
Stuffing:
¾ cup bread crumbs
¼ cup minced ham
2 tablespoons fresh chopped parsley
¼ teaspoon thyme
¼ teaspoon salt
  dash pepper
1 tablespoon lemon juice
1 teaspoon grated lemon rind
½ teaspoon chopped chives
1 egg, lightly beaten

2 tablespoons butter
3 slices bacon, chopped
1 medium onion, sliced
1 bay leaf
3 sprigs parsley
2 cups chicken stock

Combine ingredients for stuffing. Stuff birds with mixture and truss. In a large heavy pot heat butter and sauté bacon with onions for a few minutes. Add pigeons, bay leaf, 3 sprigs parsley, and 2 cups chicken stock. Bring to a boil, reduce heat, cover, and cook for about 35 to 40 minutes until tender. Transfer birds to heated serving dish and keep warm. Strain stock left in pot and reduce by half. Spoon over birds and serve with green peas and sautéed whole mushrooms.

Serves 4.

CRISPY BROILED PIGEONS

    4 pigeons, halved and flattened slightly
      salt and pepper
    1 egg, beaten
      bread crumbs
    ¼ cup melted butter
    2 tablepoons lemon juice

Season pigeon halves with salt and pepper. Dip in beaten egg and roll in bread crumbs. Sprinkle butter over pieces of pigeon and place under preheated low broiler until cooked and golden, turning a few times. Sprinkle with lemon juice and serve.

Serves 4.

CURRIED PIGEONS

4 pigeons
salt and pepper
4 tablespoons oil
4 tablespoons butter
2 tablespoons flour
2 cups milk
1 medium onion, minced
2 teaspoons curry powder or to taste
1 cup rice

Season pigeons with salt and pepper. Brown birds in heated oil. Set aside. Melt 2 tablespoons butter in saucepan; stir in flour and cook for a few minutes. Slowly pour in milk, constantly stirring, bring to a boil. Should be smooth and thick. Season well with salt and pepper. In small skillet heat remaining 2 tablespoons butter and sauté onion until transparent. Add curry powder and stir into onions. Add to sauce with browned birds and simmer for about 30 minutes. Meanwhile, cook rice according to package instructions. Form a circle of cooked rice on serving dish and put pigeons in center. Ladle curry over birds. Garnish with fresh chopped parsley and serve with chutney.

Serves 4.

FRIED PIGEONS

4 pigeons, cut in half
flour for dredging
¾ cup melted butter
4 tablespoons oil
4 slices bacon, chopped
red currant jelly

Dip pigeons in melted butter and dredge in flour. Heat oil and fry pigeons with chopped bacon until golden on both sides. Serve with red currant jelly.

Serves 4.

PIGEONS WITH WHITE WINE

2 pigeons
4 tablespoons butter
1 medium-large onion, sliced
¼ cup cooked tongue, diced
½ cup dry white wine
½ cup chicken stock
salt and pepper to taste
dash nutmeg
2 cups fresh shelled peas

Melt the butter in medium heavy saucepan. Brown birds on all sides, add onion and tongue and cook for 5 minutes. Arrange pigeons breast side up. Pour in wine and stock. Season with salt, pepper, and nutmeg. Cover and simmer for 1 hour and 15 minutes. Add peas, replace lid and cook for 15 minutes more.

Serves 2.

SQUAB

Squabs are baby pigeons. They are expensive, but splendid fare for a dinner party. Allow 1 bird per person.

CASSEROLE OF SQUAB

4 squabs
2 cups cooked wild rice mixture
2 tablespoons minced mushrooms
1 tablespoon fresh chopped parsley
4 slices bacon
5 tablespoons butter
¼ cup sherry
2 cups canned tiny peas
1 medium onion, sliced
salt and pepper to taste

Blend cooked wild rice mixture, mushrooms, and parsley. Stuff squabs, sew opening closed, and tie legs together. Wrap slice of bacon around each bird over the breast and secure with toothpick. Melt 3 tablespoons butter in baking dish, add sherry, and bring to a boil. Set squabs in mixture and place baking dish in 375°F. oven for 25 minutes. Baste squabs often with sauce in dish. Meanwhile, sauté onion in 2 tablespoons butter for 5 minutes. When squabs have cooked 20 minutes, add peas and onions, season with salt and pepper. Cook 10 to 15 minutes more.

Serves 3 or 4.

SAUTÉED SQUAB WITH WINE SAUCE

        4 squabs, halved
           salt and pepper
        2 tablespoons butter
        2 tablespoons oil
    1½ tablespoons flour
        1 cup chicken stock
    ½ cup red wine

Season squab halves with salt and pepper. Melt butter with oil in large skillet and brown squabs on all sides, a few halves at a time, adding equal amounts of butter and oil if needed. As squabs are browned, transfer to side dish. Sprinkle flour in skillet. While stirring, add chicken stock and wine. Bring to a boil. Season well with salt and pepper. Return squabs to sauce, cover and simmer 12 minutes or until squabs are tender.

Serves 4.

ROAST STUFFED SQUABS WITH PORT

4 squabs
2 tablespoons butter
6 shallots, chopped
1½ cups cooked wild rice
½ cup pistachio nuts
salt and pepper
4 bacon slices
½ cup port

Sauté shallots in butter for 5 minutes, stirring often. Combine with rice and nuts. Season with salt and pepper. Stuff squabs. Lay slice of bacon over each squab breast and secure with toothpick. Tie legs together. Roast in preheated 400°F. oven about 15 minutes. Pour port into roasting pan and cook 10 minutes longer, basting often.

Serves 2 to 4.

SQUAB PIE

4 squabs, split in half
3 tablespoons butter
¼ cup brandy
½ cup chopped ham
10 small onions
1 tablespoon fresh chopped parsley
1 tablespoon flour
½ cup Burgundy
½ cup chicken stock
salt and pepper
pastry dough for 9 inch piecrust

Melt butter in large skillet and brown squabs on both sides, cover, and simmer for 15 minutes. Pour in brandy, heat, and ignite. When flame goes out add ham, onions, and parsley. Sprinkle with flour and stir. Add wine and broth. Bring to a boil, reduce heat and simmer for 3 or 4 minutes. Season with salt and pepper. Place in pie-shaped baking dish or casserole. Cover with rolled out pastry dough ⅛ inch thick. Crimp edges of crust to dish. Bake in preheated 350°F. oven about 35 minutes until crust is golden.

Serves 4.

❧❦❧

GAME BIRDS

Game birds are an exceptionally tasty treat and one no longer has to wait for father to a-hunting-go in order to have the likes of: guinea hen, partridge, grouse, pheasant, quail, or wild duck. Such birds are now available, packaged frozen, in many specialty markets. Some people have been afraid to try these birds because of preconceived ideas about their "gamey" flavor. My advice is to try them—one serving of any of the recipes that follow should convince such timid souls of their folly.

Game birds have little fat on them, so to keep them moist while cooking place a small piece of butter inside the bird and bard with a slice of bacon or fat tied over the breast.

Fried bread crumbs and watercress provide just the right garnish.

GUINEA HEN

FRICASSEE OF GUINEA HEN

1 3½-pound guinea hen, cut into serving pieces
  flour
3 tablespoons bacon dripping
1 medium onion, chopped
1 cup red wine
1 cup chicken stock
1 bay leaf
1 teaspoon paprika
  salt and pepper

Dredge guinea hen in flour and brown in bacon drippings. Add onion, red wine, stock, bay leaf, paprika, and salt and pepper to taste. Bring to a boil and simmer for 2 hours or until tender. Serve with wild rice mixture.

Serves 4.

GROUSE

ITALIAN-STYLE GROUSE

   4 grouse
   2 stalks celery, chopped
   2 carrots, chopped
   2 sprigs parsley
   1 medium onion, stuck with 2 cloves
   1 garlic clove, minced
   ½ teaspoon salt
     dash pepper
   2 cups chicken stock
   2 cups cooked macaroni or noodles
     grated Parmesan cheese

Truss birds and place in casserole with celery, carrots, parsley, onion, garlic, salt, pepper, and chicken broth. Bring to a boil, cover, and place in 350°F. oven for 1½ hours. Remove birds to serving dish on which hot, cooked macaroni is arranged. Sprinkle grated Parmesan cheese liberally over birds. Strain sauce and pour a little over birds.

Serves 4.

ROAST GROUSE

4 grouse
4 slices bacon
  butter
  flour
4 slices toast

Truss birds, and wrap slice of bacon over each breast and secure with toothpick. Roast in preheated 425°F. oven for 30 to 35 minutes, basting often with butter. About 5 minutes before birds are done, remove bacon and dust breasts with flour and return to oven. Should be nicely browned. Serve each bird on slice of toast. Accompany with grouse giblet gravy.

Serves 4.

WILD DUCK

A BRACE OF ROAST WILD DUCKS

2 2-pound wild ducks
6 tablespoons butter
1½ cups sliced onions
½ cup chopped celery
1 teaspoon dried sage
2 tablespoons fresh chopped parsley
2 wild duck livers
½ cup bread crumbs
1 teaspoon salt
oil

Melt butter and sauté onions and celery for 5 minutes. Combine with sage, parsley, finely chopped duck livers, bread crumbs, and ½ teaspoon salt for stuffing. Dry ducks inside and out and sprinkle ¼ teaspoon salt inside each bird. Divide stuffing in half and fill birds. Sew opening closed and truss birds. Rub ducks liberally with oil. Place in preheated 450°F. oven for 30 minutes. Reduce heat to 350°F. and roast 25 to 30 minutes more until done. Serve brace of ducks on heated platter surrounded by Brussels sprouts and roast potatoes.

Serves 4.

ROAST WILD DUCK

(Mallard or teal can be used in this recipe)

    2 wild ducks
      salt and pepper
    1 apple, sliced
    1 orange, cut into ¼-inch slices
    2 celery stalks, quartered
    1 medium onion, halved
    ¼ cup dry sherry
    ¼ cup bacon drippings

Wash and dry ducks. Season cavities with salt and pepper. Combine apple, orange, celery, onion, and sherry. Divide mixture and fill each bird. Sew opening closed and tie legs together. Brush each bird with bacon drippings. Place in preheated 450°F. oven for 15 minutes on one side. Reduce heat to 350° F. and turn ducks on other side, basting with bacon drippings. After 15 minutes turn breast side up and roast ½ hour longer, basting again. Birds should cook about 1 hour all together. Remove trussing strings and cut birds in half. Discard stuffing.

Serves 4.

ROAST WILD DUCK WITH TARRAGON AND LIVER STUFFING

- 1 5-pound duck
  salt and pepper
- 3 tablespoons butter
- 1 duck liver
- 4 chicken livers
- 4 ounces liver pâté
- 1 teaspoon dried tarragon
- 3 cups bread cubes
- 2 tablespoons flour
- 1 cup duck stock
- ½ cup dry white wine

Pat duck dry and season with salt and pepper inside and out. Set aside while preparing stuffing. Sauté duck liver and chicken livers in butter for 4 or 5 minutes. Cool and chop coarsely. Mix liver pâté, chopped liver, and tarragon. Blend with bread cubes. Season with salt and pepper. Stuff duck and sew opening closed. Roast in preheated 325°F. oven for 2 to 2½ hours. Remove ducks to platter. Pour off all but 3 tablespoons duck drippings and stir in flour, scraping up browned particles in pan. Pour in 1 cup strained duck stock and wine. Bring to a boil, stirring constantly. Season with salt and pepper. Pour a little gravy over duck and serve rest in gravy boat.

Serves 4.

PARTRIDGE

HUNTER-STYLE PARTRIDGE

4 partridges, split
3 to 5 tablespoons butter, or as needed
1 medium onion, chopped
1 rounded tablespoon diced green pepper
1 large carrot, minced
1 teaspoon fresh chopped parsley
½ teaspoon thyme
1½ tablespoons flour
1½ cups chicken broth
½ cup Madeira
1 cup fresh mushrooms, diced
salt and pepper to taste

Melt 3 tablespoons butter in large Dutch oven and brown several partridge halves at a time. Add more butter if necessary. As partridges are browned transfer to side dish. Then add onion, green pepper, carrot, parsley, and thyme to butter and sauté for 4 or 5 minutes. Sprinkle flour in pan and, stirring constantly, slowly pour in chicken broth and Madeira. Place partridges in sauce. Add mushrooms and season lightly with salt and pepper. Cover and simmer for 20 to 25 minutes until partridges are tender. Serve each partridge half on slice of toast with crusts trimmed off.

Serves 4.

PARTRIDGE IN CASSEROLE
SPANISH STYLE

4 partridges
3 tablespoons olive oil
⅓ cup water
1 medium onion, chopped
2 carrots, chopped
1 small green pepper, chopped
1 leek, chopped
¼ teaspoon thyme
1 bay leaf
salt and pepper to taste
1 medium tomato, peeled, seeded, and
    chopped fine
1 teaspoon white vinegar
1 tablespoon flour

Wash and pat dry partridges. Truss each bird. Heat olive oil and brown partridges on all sides. Place partridges breast side up in casserole and add water, onion, carrots, green pepper, leek, thyme, bay leaf, and salt and pepper. Cover and simmer for 35 to 40 minutes until tender. Transfer partridges to heated serving dish and cover to keep warm. Strain sauce and pour into clean saucepan. Add tomato, vinegar, flour and whisk until sauce thickens slightly. Remove trussing string from birds, and pour sauce over birds. Surround partridges with rice and garnish with fresh parsley.

Serves 4.

PARTRIDGE ON SAUERKRAUT

2 partridges
salt and pepper
2 slices bacon
4 tablespoons butter
1 tablespoon oil
½ cup minced carrots
2 tablespoons minced shallots
¼ cup chicken stock
1 tablespoon flour
2 cups sauerkraut
¾ cup white wine
¼ cup heavy cream

Season birds with salt and pepper. Wrap slice of bacon around each bird over breast and secure with toothpick. Melt 2 tablespoons butter with oil and brown birds on all sides. Add carrots, shallots, chicken stock and bring to a boil. Cover and simmer for 25 to 30 minutes. Turn birds once during cooking. Meanwhile, place sauerkraut in colander and rinse with water and drain. Melt remaining 2 tablespoons butter in skillet. Add wine. Bring to a boil and add sauerkraut. Blend, cover, and simmer for 30 minutes. Add extra chicken broth if too dry. Transfer birds to heated dish and keep warm. Sprinkle flour over sauce in pan where partridges cooked, and blend. Add cream and bring to a boil. Cook for 3 minutes, whisking often. Season, strain, and serve in sauceboat. Cut partridges in half and place on bed of sauerkraut. Ladle sauce over each bird.

Serves 2.

PARTRIDGE WITH WHITE GRAPES

2 partridges, washed, dried, and trussed
3 slices bacon, chopped
2 tablespoons butter
¼ cup white wine
¼ cup fresh chopped parsley
  pinch of thyme
1 bay leaf
1 stalk celery, cut in half
1 leek, cut in half
3 cups firm white grapes
  salt and pepper to taste

Cook pieces of bacon until crisp and reserve for garnish. Brown partridges in bacon fat with butter, then add remaining ingredients including grapes, cover and simmer for 1 hour. Serve partridge surrounded by grapes and garnish with cooked crumbled bacon.

Serves 2.

ROAST PARTRIDGE

4 partridges
  salt and pepper
4 slices bacon
  flour
¾ cup chicken stock
5 tablespoons butter
1 cup bread crumbs

Season partridges lightly inside and out with salt and pepper. Truss and wrap slice of bacon around each breast. Place in preheated 425°F. oven and roast for 25 to 30 minutes. Remove bacon and dust birds lightly with flour. Return to oven and cook 5 minutes more until birds brown nicely. Transfer to heated serving dish and keep hot. Add chicken stock to pan and bring to a boil, scraping up roasting particles collected on bottom of pan. Season well. Swirl in 2 tablespoons butter, strain, and pour over birds. Serve with bread crumbs fried in 3 tablespoons butter.

Serves 4.

PHEASANT

PHEASANT—HUNTER STYLE

 2 pheasants, cut into serving pieces
¼ cup flour
 1 teaspoon salt
   pepper to taste
 1 teaspoon paprika
 2 tablespoons oil
 4 tablespoons butter
¼ pound mushrooms, quartered
 2 medium onions, chopped
 1 clove garlic, crushed
½ green pepper, chopped
 1 bay leaf, crushed
 2 cups canned tomatoes and liquid
 1 teaspoon lemon juice
½ cup dry white wine

Combine flour, salt, pepper, and paprika. Dredge cut-up pheasant in seasoned flour. Melt 2 tablespoons butter with oil and brown pheasant several pieces at a time. Transfer pheasant to side dish. Add 2 tablespoons remaining butter to pan and cook mushrooms, onions, garlic, and green peppers for 5 minutes. Add bay leaf, lemon juice, tomatoes, and crush tomatoes with fork. Pour in white wine and bring to a boil. Return pheasant to pan, cover, and simmer for 45 minutes or until tender.

Serves 6.

PHEASANT LUCULLUS

1 pheasant
1 cup flour seasoned with salt and pepper
1 tablespoon oil
2 tablespoons butter
2 onions, sliced
½ pound mushrooms, sliced
⅔ cup Madeira
¼ pound ham cut into julienne strips
    bouquet garni of: 3 sprigs parsley, 1 stalk
       celery cut in half, 1 bay leaf, 6 peppercorns,
     1 leek, and good pinch of thyme
    salt and pepper to taste
1 tablespoon truffle juice (optional)
1 tablespoon each butter and flour

Cut pheasant into serving pieces. Dredge in flour and fry in heated oil and butter until golden on both sides. Remove and keep warm. Sauté the sliced onions for 10 minutes in butter and add mushrooms. Pour wine in and add ham and bouquet garni. Season with salt and pepper. Put pheasant pieces back in pan and pour in truffle juice if used. Cover and simmer slowly. Pheasant should sit on top of ingredients. Put in slow oven, 300°F. for 1½ to 2 hours. Turn pheasant pieces occasionally. Add a little stock if necessary. Remove bouquet garni and discard. Blend 1 tablespoon each of butter and flour. Dissolve in simmering sauce on top of stove and cook for a few minutes longer. Garnish with fresh chopped parsley.

Serves 3 to 4.

PHEASANT NORMANDY

1 2½-pound pheasant
3 tablespoons butter
3 tart cooking apples, peeled, cored, and sliced
¼ cup Calvados (apple brandy) or Cognac
¾ cup heavy cream
  pinch nutmeg
  salt and pepper

Melt butter in casserole and brown trussed pheasant on all sides. Remove pheasant from pan. Add apples and sauté for 5 minutes. Transfer apples to side dish and return pheasant to pan. Pour Calvados over pheasant, heat, and ignite. Pour heavy cream over pheasant and surround with apples. Season with salt, pepper, and nutmeg. Cover and simmer for about 45 minutes. Remove pheasant and carve. Place apple mixture on heated serving dish and arrange pheasant on top. Pour sauce over pheasant.

Serves 2.

PHEASANT UNDER GLASS

Any dish served under glass immediately becomes romantic and elegant. It is a cooking method rarely seen today and that is too bad because the delicate flavor it produces is especially enticing and unusual. Pheasant Under Glass is the most famous dish in the under-glass category, although many different foods can be deliciously cooked in this manner.

2 baby pheasants
3 tablespoons butter
1 tablespoon oil
2 slices bacon
1 tablespoon chopped parsley
1 garlic clove, minced
1 teaspoon lemon juice
2 tablespoons white wine

Truss pheasants and season lightly with salt and pepper. Melt butter with oil in skillet and brown birds on all sides. Place each bird in buttered individual baking dish. Cover each pheasant with slice of bacon which has been blanched in boiling water for 3 minutes. Pour 1 tablespoon browning fat over each bird and sprinkle with equal amounts of parsley, garlic, lemon juice, and wine. Cover each with glass bell and bake in preheated 350°F. oven for 50 to 55 minutes until tender.

Serves 2.

QUAIL

CASSEROLE OF QUAILS
WITH PEAS

8 quails
1½ sticks butter
1 clove garlic, minced
½ cup chicken broth
2 cups peas
1 medium zucchini, diced
1 medium onion, chopped fine
salt and pepper

Place 1 tablespoon butter inside each quail, and tie legs together. Melt 2 tablespoons butter in large casserole and add quails. Season with salt, pepper, and minced garlic. Place in preheated 425°F. oven for 15 minutes. Meanwhile, bring broth to a boil, add peas, zucchini, onion, and 2 tablespoons butter. Season with salt and pepper, cover, and simmer 8 minutes. Transfer to casserole and cook with quails for 3 minutes longer.

Serves 4.

QUAILS IN PORT

   8 quails
   8 slices bacon
   8 slices day old white bread
   6 tablespoons butter or as needed
   1 cup port
     salt and pepper
   4 ounces foie gras

Truss and wrap each bird with slice of bacon. Roast in preheated 425°F. oven for 20 minutes. Meanwhile, trim crusts from bread, melt butter, and fry bread on both sides until golden. Transfer cooked quail to a heated dish and keep hot. Pour port in roasting pan and bring to a boil. Swirl in 2 tablespoons butter and season with salt and pepper. Spread fried bread with foie gras, and place one quail on each. Pour sauce over quails and serve.

Serves 4.

QUAIL OVEN-FRIED

   8 quails
   2 eggs, beaten with 1 tablespoon water
   1 cup dried bread crumbs
   1 tablespoon chervil
   1 tablespoon salt
  ½ teaspoon fresh ground pepper
   4 tablespoons butter
   2 tablespoons oil

Secure legs of each quail together with string, and dip each quail in beaten egg and water mixture. Blend together bread crumbs, chervil, salt and pepper. Roll quails in flavored crumbs. Melt butter with oil, and brown quails on all sides, a few at a time. Place browned quails in baking dish or pan, cover with foil and bake in preheated 400°F. oven for about 20 minutes.

Serves 4.

QUAIL THYME

    4 quails
      salt and pepper to taste
    4 tablespoons butter
    1 tablespoon chopped shallots
    1 tablespoon flour
    ½ teaspoon dried thyme
    ½ cup dry white wine
    ½ cup beef stock

Season birds with salt and pepper, and truss. Melt butter, and brown birds on all sides over medium-high heat. Reduce heat to a simmer. Add shallots and cook 5 minutes. Sprinkle flour over birds and turn them. Add thyme, white wine, and beef stock. Bring to a boil, reduce heat, cover, and simmer for 10 to 15 minutes. Place birds in heated serving dish and pour sauce over them.

Serves 2.

ROAST QUAIL

8 quails
8 slices of bacon
    butter for basting
8 slices white toast, crusts trimmed off

Tie legs of birds together. Bard each quail by wrapping a slice of bacon over breast of bird and securing with toothpick. Place in roasting pan and roast in preheated 425°F. oven for about 15 to 20 minutes. Baste often with butter. Serve each quail on slice of toasted white bread that has been spread with butter.

Serves 4.

SAUTÉED QUAILS IN CREAM SAUCE

6 quails, cut in half
    salt and pepper
    paprika
3 tablespoons butter
2 tablespoons oil
2 medium onions, chopped
1 clove garlic, crushed
⅔ cup heavy cream
1 tablespoon sherry

Season quail with salt, pepper, and paprika. Melt butter with oil in large skillet, and brown quail. Add onions, garlic, and cook for 2 minutes. Pour in heavy cream and sherry. Cover and simmer 20 to 25 minutes until tender.

Serves 3 to 4.

INDEX